ACTUALLY, LACAN II
On Free Association

Translations by Andrea Zorzutti

Cuerno Verde Press
Printing House Of
Colorado Analytic Forum of the Lacanian Field
A Nonprofit 501(c)(3) Organization

Actually, Lacan II: On Free Association
Copyright © 2023 by Cuerno Verde Press
All Rights Reserved

Cover Design: Lucio Napolitano
ISBN for the print version of KDP is 978-1-961239-02-9
ISBN for the eBook version of KDP is 978-1-961239-03-6

Contents

Introduction 1

How Free is Free Association? 3
    Gabriel Lombardi

The Rule of Free Association: Free at Last? 9
    Julieta De Battista

Interpretation: From the Logic of the Signifier To the Po-et(h)ics of the Act 23
    Ana Laura Prates

Something Borrowed, Something New 37
    Matías Laje

The Structure of the Cartel as Structure and Engineering in the School: From the Gateway to the Pass, the Cartel 43
    Sonia Alberti

On the Link of Free Association and Repetition 59
    Nate Koser

The Fundamental Rule and Resistance 67
    Gabriela Zorzutti

The Impossibilities to Free Association 81
    Barbara Shuman

Free Association and Mourning 93
    Michael McAndrew

Freud's "Bias": Notes on Psychical Determinism 101
    Michael Barnard

Introduction

This is the second issue of *Actually, Lacan,* the journal of the Colorado Analytic Forum of the Lacanian Field. The first issue appeared in 2015 and included a number of distinguished writers and Lacanian analysts from Latin America. It is indicative of the Colorado Forum's continuing camaraderie with forums of the southern hemisphere, especially in Argentina, that a few of those same authors have generously consented to appear here once again, including Gabriel Lombardi, Matia Laje, and Gabriela Zorzutti – who in particular seems to straddle both American hemispheres of the Lacanian world.

Joining them this time are three equally distinguished writers and analysts who we've invited and are excited to present in these pages, namely Sonia Alberti, Julieta De Battista, and Ana Laura Prates. Each of them has published widely on a variety of psychoanalytic topics in Spanish, or in the case of Dr. Alberti in Portuguese, German, English and French.

Finally, we have selected essays that were submitted by Colorado Forum members Michael Barnard, Nate Koser, Michael McAndrew, Barbara Shuman, and Gabriela Zorzutti.

It should be noted from the onset that, while Lacan is an undeniable presence in America's academic realm, the essays that follow were written by practitioners of Lacanian analysis. We have followed Lacan's own example in our intention to address this work to practicing analysts and analysts-in-formation. We invite anyone else with the desire and capacity to peer in as well, as it were, through the portals of the unconscious.

The theme we have chosen for the essays in this new issue of *Actually, Lacan* is once again firmly and most intentionally clinical in orientation. Free association as governed by the fundamental rule – urging to "say whatever you want to say," while also instructing to "say especially whatever you would rather not say" – was chosen precisely because this practice is what defines and distinguishes psychoanalysis from therapies that would foster the ego and reeducate the drives.

The Editors, *Cuerno Verde Press*

How Free is Free Association?

Gabriel Lombardi

The history of the word *association* does not help to imagine freedom, since it comes from the Latin *sequi*, to follow. *Socius* is the one that follows another, *signum* is the signal that is followed, as seen in *sign*, *signature* and other such related terms that English borrowed from Latin. What we call *signifier* implies for its subject a compulsion to find what it means, what it represents or vectorizes, and with even greater force when it appears isolated, loose, detached, dissociated. The signifier demands association, it orders to give him a *socius*, a partner, a signification, at least another signifier.

Associationism was born long before Freud. Already the Greeks, Aristotle of course, and Diogenes Laertius, among others, noticed that ideas and concepts are associated following certain rules: by similarity, by contrast, by contiguity, by composition. Hobbes, Locke, and especially David Hartley before Hume, James, and John Stuart Mill founded British Associationism, in which laws of sequential ordering and composition of sensations, memories, ideas, and mental processes were elaborated. What characterizes this classical school is that association processes are studied as automatic ones, following determined general laws, preparing the ground for the robotic inspiration that predominates in current neuropsychology in its cognitive and behavioral aspects. According to this angle – which adapts very well to digital capitalism, as rats, robots, and humans share common patterns –, behaviors can be tracked and then programmed, their affinities and routes can be predicted by algorithms. Associations are calculable or at least are locatable elements.

Contrary to the idea that the human being is the passive result of a net or rhizomatic node of associations ruled by general laws, the Freudian contribution was in another direction. The hypothesis of a particular unconscious, inaccessible to common laws, is based on the resistance of human patients to display associative automatisms.

Indeed, while Freud admits that there is in all of us a compulsion to the association, at the same time he wonders to what extent there is an essential moment of freedom, an instance that resists all external induction or internal programming of associations. He surveys for instance to what extent in the associations of his hysterical patients there were some elective moments. He explores the same subject in the associations that dreams give rise to and in those that are condensed or displaced in a *lapsus linguae*, a forgetfulness of proper nouns or other bungled actions. The Freudian hypothesis of the unconscious grants for the human being a structural existential factor or condition that differs from that of the rat or the robot; let's call it desire, the unconscious, an indestructible desire discerned by Freud. The initial purpose of the A.I. is to introduce such a component into the machine.

That is why Freud begins his research with a fundamental methodological step, based on what he calls free association. He quickly finds that the associations are not unequivocal, that white, as for the Eskimos, can express 37 different shades, and that white is also milk, egg white, sclera, fresh semen, and some drugs. In the logical language of our days, we can say that Freud anticipates that the equivocality of language guarantees the aptitude of association as truly free, because the transfinite order of the possible associative combinations of human language overcomes any pretense of algorithmic determination. This was demonstrated in 1931 by a certain Kurt Gödel.

This enormous capability of equivocality of human language makes possible the particularity of the symptom, the singularity of each destiny and even that poetry that allows Lady Macbeth, on a bloody night, to say to her husband: "My hands are of your color, but I shame to wear a heart so white."

Freud introduces a vital touch into the theories of the association through the dynamic of the dispute in which both his fundamental theoretical notions and his clinical concepts are constituted and activated. The overdetermining *unconscious* scoffs at regulated associative constraints, *repetition* prevents new associations, *transference* is a resistance to the free association method, the *drive* dissociates itself from any planned representation of its object. In the same way, *inhibition*, as an affair of the Ego, ignores the unconscious and prevents association; *anguish* actively signals the radical lack of a signifier to associate with; the *symptom* is the elective discomfort of the speaking being when it, being able to choose freely, remains oscillating on the threshold of the act.

The analytic method then encourages the "patient," who suffers from coercive, bullying representations, to become an analysand, capable of actively reproducing or inventing associations and symptoms, even if they distract about and procrastinate the words that could resolve the situation of postponed desire. An occurrence, an interpretation, however random, if he is interested in it, will not be *automatic* for him but *tychic*, lucky or unlucky, desirable or despicable. The method even encourages the release of associations from the structure of the ordered description, from the coherent discourse, from the supposedly interesting, and from moral considerations.

Lacan wrote the most precise text I have ever read on free association, "The Direction of the Cure and the Principles of its Power."[1] He explains there the diverse possible consequences of the Freudian fundamental rule and puts it in conversation with three levels of the analyst's intervention: the freedom to interpret, the maneuver of the transference by which the analyst has to get out of an abrupt or persistent restriction to that freedom, and the act in which the analyst has to pay even with his most intimate judgment to house an element that will not admit association, the *Kern unseres Wesen* that Freud situated in our intimate core. Through this triple diversification that substitutes an impossible intersubjective dialogue, the analytical process aims to free the analysand's associations to its limit. And how to situate that limit? Let us recall a key paragraph of that text.

The analyst is the man to whom one speaks and to whom one speaks freely. That is what he is there for. What does it mean? Everything that can be said about the association of ideas is mere dressing up in psychologistic clothing. Induced plays on words are far removed from it; because of their protocol, moreover, nothing could be less free.

The subject invited to speak in analysis does not really display a great deal of freedom in what he says. Not that he is bound by the rigor of his associations: they no doubt oppress him, but it is rather that they lead to a free speech, a full speech that would be painful to him.

---

[1] Lacan, Jacques. Ecrits, p. 514

Nothing is feared more than saying something that may be true. For it would become entirely true if it were said, and Lord knows what happens when something can no longer be cast into doubt because it is true.

The ironic allusion to God, the western canonical form of the subject supposed to knowledge, points out the only precise moment in which there is no Other, at least the only one that surges in the analytic experience as accomplished within the framework of a *social* bond: the moment of decision or choice by which something can be said that marks a before and an after, a real step in which words are sublimated into an act, the act of saying. It is the act of saying *yes* or *no* to what is wanted, the only performance of free will guaranteed for us. Only an elective moment can deconstruct or analyze the omniscience and prescience of the Other. Only a sin, said Boethius, a crime or misdemeanor, said Woody Allen, a tap on the drum that fires all the sounds and starts a new harmony, a new love! Rimbaud said.

We could deduce, with Lacanian tools, that the experience cast by analytical method demonstrates that all our significant associations, even all our *social* links, are based on a fundamental deficiency of association, namely the impossibility of the sexual rapport introduced in the *parlêtre* by his antinatural *progeniture*: born as we are, a product of language. In human language, sex is not representable. Sex is the Other that can't be the partner of the One. Sex, then, is not symbolic, it is real. This lack of the Other sex in the symbolic grants to us, as speaking beings, the persistence of sexual desire that precedes each act, each free choice we could perform even in its more asexual, parasexual, demisexual, generic, degenerated, or sublimated arrangements.

So, we can conceive that the core of our action is placed in the structural absence of that sexual association. That lack offers us the possibility of "free" association, with that sole precise restriction.

And that's why your daughter is mute, says Molière's physician in *The Doctor Despite Himself.*[2]

---

[2] "...Le Médecin malgré lui (Moliere, 1666; The Doctor in Spite of Himself), which begins as a farce based on the simple joke of mistaking the ne'er-do-well woodcutter Sganarelle for a doctor, gradually becomes a satire on learned pretension and bourgeois credulity." Ed. (Britannica)

The Rule of Free Association: Free at Last?

Julieta De Battista

The fundamental nature of the rule

In "The Direction of the Cure and the Principles of its Power,"[3] Lacan emphasizes that, initially, the direction of the cure is all about the patient we receive applying the fundamental rule. This is the condition of entry to the analytical experience.

The experience is therefore constituted by this first step: to free the saying from the chains of the story, coherence, and criticism. To submit it instead to something that is much more difficult to bear: the law of non-omission and the law of non-systematization, through which it is to be assumed that all the debris of mental life can be valuable (Lacan, 1936).

To open the door to this incoherence, to this powdery discourse – to this saying whatever, without hesitating to say nonsense – is the fundamental step to enter the analytic experience.[4] It is the unbearable step at the beginning, since, if the potential analysand has to be invited to such an undertaking, it is because he does not have such freedom.

The analyst is there to be talked to in this way. How does he get the patient to take this fundamental step?

In this regard, I would like to comment on an aspect that Lacan highlights in 1958, which is the following: it is in the inflections, in

---

[3] Lacan, Jaques. *Ecrits*
[4] (Lacan, 1972-1973)

how the analyst achieves the application of this rule, that we will discover in what way the analyst's doctrine of the analytical situation is transmitted and the "point of consequence" it has reached for him (Lacan, 1958: 586). This would allow us to suppose that the way of enunciating and enforcing this fundamental rule could undergo changes according to the point that the doctrinal elaboration has reached, but also, I add, the experience of one's own analysis for one who listens to it. It follows then that the pass from analysand to analyst has an impact on the enunciation of the rule, on how someone is compelled to enter the analyzing task. This "point of consequence" that an analysis may have reached can be very diverse, even for concluded analyses. We know that there are analyses that culminate in the accomplishment of certain therapeutic effects, that others continue a step further until they grasp the flaw in the Subject Supposed to Knowledge, but also that there are other analyses that, having reached this point, go no further in the mourning[5] of the end that would allow the separation from the analyst. And yet, we know that there are analyses that have reached said mourning, that have come out of it, and that have not produced a wish to take the place of the analyst. So, the destinations and the ends of analysis are most varied.

I wonder what changes with respect to the fundamental rule at the end of analysis. Analyses begin with free association and continue on that road, but do they break up with it? Free association may seem very elementary, but it is the one condition that the analyst must enforce: from the way in which he enunciates and sustains it, the direction of the cure will emerge, the way in which an attempt is made to circumscribe the singular from the particular

---

[5] T.N. The original *duelo* means both mourning and duel.

of the symptom. What does the end of analysis, or more precisely, the encounter with the fate of the desire of the analyst, contribute to the enunciation of this rule? Will there be differences between those who have only finished their analyses and those who have found themselves becoming analysts? Is there a singular stamp obtained from the analytical journey? Does an analyst relaunch this rule even at the end or does he drop it? Can an analyst influence the "infinitization" of an analysis? Is there some "liberation" at the end? I will not be able to respond to all these questions but I sustain the importance of stating them, at least.

The opening act

The conquest of some tactical freedom is not enough to onset the analytical experience. The production of an analyst is not just about being good at playing with words. The knowledge of the analyst is not a tactical knowledge of how to intervene according to the logic of the case. It's not that. What operates in an analysis is the desire of the analyst, sustained by politics and a strategy in which this tactical freedom takes place, without forgetting that there is no such freedom in the politics of analysis. Lacan approaches this knowledge of the analyst saying, first, that it is the knowledge of impotence, it is not a supposed knowledge, it is an expired knowledge , to specify it later as the knowledge to be waste.[6] This is what lies at the beginning, and this is what lies at the end.

I believe this is in solidarity to the three payments that Lacan mentions for the analyst: he pays with his words, he pays with his person, but above all, he pays with his innermost judgment. What free-speaking could be sustained if the analyst did not pay each and

---

[6] (Lacan, 1973)

every time with his innermost judgment? The analyst is someone capable of not being affected by everything a human being says, someone who does not resort to "I like it" or "I don't like it."[7] Some analysands locate very well how there were things that remained undiscussed with this or that analyst because that analyst would have been horrified, or would not have been able to hear it, or was too naive to understand it, or his political position prevented him! We could reply with Lacan: "The analyst is the man to whom one speaks and to whom one speaks freely. That's what he is there for."[8]

Now, to be there simply for that, he also needs to pay. What are the reasons that lead an analyst to agree to meet these many payments? Undoubtedly, we cannot close this question simply by saying "he charges good money." There will be other reasons. The question is which ones in each case.

Going back to the beginning, the fundamental rule is an invitation to lose the thread while speaking and this is neither an ideal requirement nor a superego requirement, nor does it aim at obtaining merely a resistive obedience: it is the essential ethical condition of the analytical experience. How is this rule enforced? Each analyst will find his style to promote its continuity, in act he will try to rescue that which is about to be omitted, silenced. Each analyst finds his way, or not, to give the rule the fundamental weight he thinks it has in the experience.

This inaugural act belongs to the analyst, the act of enforcing the rule opens up a new field, someone is invited to lose the thread, and, in losing himself, to find himself again. The act is on the side of the analyst and the doing on that of the analysand (Lacan, 1967-

---

[7] (Lacan, 1967-1968: 102).
[8] (Lacan, 1958: 616).

1968). The original and inaugural act is on the analyst's part. Hence, Lacan's question is about the conditions for the production of an analyst, for if one analyst exists, "all is secured, there can be many more."[9]

The rule is the royal road, it is the fundamental alliance with the experience of the unconscious, it is a way to "dismiss the subject"[10] and let the signifier play its game, appear in its power, in act. A dismissal of the subject is already in operation in the enunciation of the rule, to which the analytic act gives its statute. The task of the analysand implies it.[11]

Analysands have various ways of devaluing their saying, trying to maintain coherence and justify their omissions — "it's nonsense, I'm embarrassed, I can't say it, it's beside the point, I wasn't going to tell it." They also have their ways of slipping in some crucial fancy at the end of the session, at a time when the analyst does not seem to be paying attention, saying it on the quiet, in passing, or stopping and censoring, leaving certain ellipses.

The rule will have its chance of operating to the extent that there be an analyst willing to pay with his innermost judgment and to enforce it. An analyst asserts the fundamental rule at the exact instant when shame threatens to authorize the omission, in the precise moment when the aspiration of coherence stops the incessant flow of unplanned speech, he insists on continuing despite that ephemeral breath that suggests "I'd better not say this, I'd better keep quiet about this." In those deleterious moments when the inaugural pact falters, it is essential for the analytical task

---

[9] (Lacan, 1967-1968).
[10] (Lacan, 1968-1969)
[11] (Lacan, 1967-1968: 64).

that the analyst responds: "continue, go ahead, go on, what were you going to say?"

The analysand's doing is established by the act of the analyst. It is in this conjunction that the dispositif invented by Freud reveals its power (Lacan, 1967-1968). The analyst remains as in a crouching position, attentively waiting for what the analysand's doing is able to produce.[12] The analysand is the subject who does. This doing is on the analyst's side. An analyst does not fall into the "irresistible temptation to do."[13] (Lacan, 1967-1968).

By his invitation to free association, the analyst incites the establishment of the Subject Supposed to Knowledge: that which is said when losing the thread, when making an effort to speak about his symptoms, "from that about which he is most unwilling to talk,"[14] this way of saying has a value for the listener, that which would be discarded in a social conversation may mean something else.

The acceptance of the rule brings about a consent to an effect of inaugural loss, namely, losing the thread when speaking. From the beginning, the experience of analysis confronts this effect of loss, and it is yet to be seen how willing the analysand is to this…as well as the analyst.

This distinction between the analysand's doing and the analytic act is essential. Lacan remembers that "the efficiency of the act has nothing to do with the effectiveness of doing."[15] The beginning of analysis is an act of the analyst, that of inviting into the fundamental rule, that of asserting this saying. This analytic act incites

---

[12](Lacan, 1967-1968)
[13](Lacan, 1967-1968)
[14](Lacan, 1975a: 24)
[15] Lacan (1967-1968)

knowledge, while accepting to be the support of this Subject Supposed to Knowledge that is, as we know, destined to *desêtre*.

The analysand is not the only one who may resist the fundamental rule, the analyst can also resist it. Ignorance of the analytic act is typical of analysts! One of the appearances of resistance is to leave the path of the act and enter the path of doing.

The act at the end

The inaugural enunciation of the rule incites the Subject Supposed to Knowledge and is founded in this position. "Say anything, whatever comes up, whatever crosses your mind, without criticism or omissions," this will have value for the Other. In this way transference is established, supported by the analyst. If the analyst does not resist the analysand's doing too much, the turns of free association will gradually reveal his unconscious determinisms: that of which he is a prisoner, and what security he obtained therein.

The function of the analyst institutes this doing with a purpose that is not just the playful "infinitization" of free association. All those turns of free association, of this dropping what exceeds conscience, are drilling on something, producing an erosion that writes. Where does this way of talking to an analyst lead? "It is not at all about leading someone to make a name or creating a work of art. It is something that consists in inciting [someone] to pass through the good hole of that which is offered as singular."[16]

So, the analyst lets the analysand do, but until when? Until the fall of that to which he was incited occurs, until the failure of the Subject Supposed to Knowledge is grasped. There is always one more round for associations, so what stops this infernal whirlwind,

---

[16](Lacan, 1975a: 24)

which revolves around the hole of the non-sexual-relationship and whose position is at stake in those edges before the impossible? Inciting knowledge by the artifice of the fundamental rule leads to a knowledge that produces the *object a*: "The *a* comes to substitute the opening designated in the impasse of the sexual relationship."[17] The *object a* is the waste of these turns of knowledge; it is the cause of the desire at the beginning of the act.[18]

At the end of the analysis this *object a* is evacuated, and it is the object that the analyst will come to represent: the analyst falls. "He himself becomes the rejected fiction."[19] So, the required effect of analytic discourse is neither imaginary nor symbolic: it is real, the real of an effect of meaning.[20] This effect of meaning ex-sists and in this it is real. It emerges from the rejection of all the fiction that was propitiated via the fundamental rule.

Another kind of silence appears then, a musicality different from silence, a silence different from the others that have inhabited the cure: it is not the silence of resistance, nor that of surprise, or shame, or omission. It is perhaps a silence that can only be heard at the threshold of loneliness, when the echo and the resonances of saying go quiet, when something of the *jouissance* of speaking "freely" is sacrificed. A driven silence that pushes towards something else. Not in vain did Robert Fliess link the different forms of silence to erogenous body orifices.[21] Maybe an invoking silence can emerge in the end, calling for another destination. In 1975 Lacan resumes

---

[17](Lacan, 1968-1969: 347)

[18](Lacan, 1967-1968)

[19](Lacan, 1968-1969: 348)

[20] **Lacan, 1974-1975)**

[21] Fliess, R. (1949). Silence and verbalization: a supplement to the theory of the "analytic rule." The international Journal of Psychoanalysis, XXX

the writing of the analytic discourse and says that silence corresponds to the semblant of waste, which he places as an agent (Lacan, 1975b: 63). This does not mean that the analyst must remain silent, but precisely that he must emphasize the articulation between this silence that exceeds the analysand's doing and its relationship with the semblant of waste.

The analyst is destined to lose, to be eliminated from the process of which he was the cause.[22] His position is made up "substantially" of the *object a* and this object designates an effect in discourse that is an "effect of rejection" (Lacan, 1969-1970: 47). The analyst represents the effect of rejection in discourse, that is to say, the *object a*. (Lacan, 1969-1970): "(...) of that which I introduce as the new order in the world I must become the waste" (Lacan, 1967-1968). Where it was, the waste may come.

Rejection is what the analyst is destined for in his act, the rejected rock that is transformed during the analysis from serving as the cornerstone.[23] A paradox about the analytic act emerges from this, which Lacan points out: "If it is true that the analyst knows what an analysis is and what it leads to, how can he proceed with this act?"[24] The analyst is an actor who is erased, evacuating the *object a*. What could make someone want to fulfill such a function? What desire, what satisfaction can be found there?[25]

The question is not merely about the conditions of the end of analysis, it is a question that goes beyond, that aims at the reasons why someone that knows from the end of his own analysis what is the destination of the analyst and yet wishes to embody that

---

[22] (Lacan, 1969-1970)
[23] (Lacan, 1969-1970: 125)
[24] (Lacan, 1968-1969: 348).
[25] (Lacan, 1968-1969: 350, 351).

function. Which is to say, that not only is the knowledge of the symptom extracted from the analysis, but also a knowledge about the analyst's destination at the end of the process and something that compels one to wish to occupy this place that arises from an effect of rejection. Is there any desire, any satisfaction in particular? It would also have to be a desire or a satisfaction that allows for an exit from the dispositif, so as not to be trapped in it. For it could also happen that an analysand persists in delighting himself in the very satisfaction of having someone to talk to freely. The coordinates of this exit will be the key to sifting through those other reasons why someone who has analyzed himself sufficiently may want to pass from doing to the act: "The end was reached at one time and from there one has to deduce the relationship that this has with the beginning of every time."[26] "The best way to re-enter safely is to truly exit."[27] This paradox is of great importance for the future of psychoanalysis, it is the question of how this doing of the analysand can produce not only the end of analysis but an analytic act. Around this paradox, and his question of what is the satisfaction at play in bearing the function of the analyst, Lacan presents two important references: that of the scapegoat and the comparison of the position of the analyst with the masochistic position.

The analyst as scapegoat carries the *object a*.[28] According to the Greek origin of the word, the *pharmakos* is one who immolates himself in atonement for the faults of another; in such sacrificial rite the expiatory victim was expelled from the city and this freed the rest from their guilt. Is the analyst a modern scapegoat? Does this

---

[26] (Lacan, 1967-1968)
[27] (Lacan, 1967-1968)
[28] (Lacan, 1968-1969)

explain Lacan's insight that a community of analysts could become a society for the protection of scapegoats, who would find some "salvation" in grouping and grading?[29] If so, would there be some satisfaction in being expelled, sacrificed? Or would this be no more than a religious tint that could color the analytic practice? In the name of the father, the son, and the scapegoat!

Regarding the confrontation between the analytic act and masochistic practice Lacan warns, from the outset, that we should not confuse the one with the other. The masochist is a master of the true game, he gets *jouissance* from failing and requires the Other.[30] We do not say the same about the analyst: neither that he gets *jouissance* from failing, nor that he is a master, nor that he requires the Other. Nor do we assume that he is seeking something in particular regarding his *jouissance*: "It is where the surplus of *jouissance* was, the *jouissance* of the Other, that I, in as much as I utter the analytic act, must come to be.[31]"

Fatum

What leads, then, to the emergence of the analyst? What is it that compels him to play the role of the *object a*, with all that this means? Not sacrifice or masochism. What other reasons then? "The position of the analyst, if strictly in accordance with his act, is one where, in the field of doing that he inaugurates with the aid of this act, there is no room for whatever he dislikes – whatever it may be –, nor for what he likes. If he makes room for that, he's out."[32] In some hidden corner of the analytical journey and its destinations, and

---

[29] (Lacan, 1968-1969)
[30] (Lacan, 1968-1969)
[31] (Lacan, 1969-1970: 59)
[32] (Lacan, 1968-1969: 354)

even knowing how the game ends, some new desire propels the one who is to become an analyst to renew the trust in the fundamental rule. Beyond what I like and dislike, despite the silence, the loneliness, the expulsion, the pain and the rejection, he finds some reason, some thrust, he feels called upon to receive new cases of emergency.

Bibliography

Fliess, R. (1949). Silence and verbalization: a supplement to the theory of the `analytic rule'. *The International Journal of Psychoanalysis*, XXX.

Lacan, J. (1936). Au delà du "Principe de realité". In J. Lacan, *Écrits*, Paris: Seuil, p.73-92.

Lacan, J. (1958). La direction de la cure et les principes de son pouvoir. In J. Lacan, *Écrits*, Paris: Seuil, 585-646.

Lacan, J. (1967-1968). *Le séminaire. Livre XV. L'acte psychanalytique*. Inédito.

Lacan, J. (1968-1969). *Le séminaire. Livre XVI. D'un Autre à l'autre*. Paris: Seuil.

Lacan, J. (1969-1970). *Le séminaire. Livre XVII. L'envers de la psychanalyse*. Paris: Seuil.

Lacan, J. (1971-1972). *Le séminaire. Livre XIX. ...ou pire*. Paris: Seuil.

Lacan, J. (1972-1973) *Le séminaire. Livre XX. Encore*. Paris: Seuil.

Lacan, J. (1973). Note italienne. In J. Lacan. *Autres écrits*. Paris: Seuil, p. 307-312.

Lacan, J. (1974-1975). *Le séminaire. Livre XXII. RSI*. Inédito.

Lacan, J. (1975a). Intervention à la suite de l'exposé de André Albert sur le plaisir et la règle fondamentale. Journées d'étude de l'EFP de juin 1975, *Lettres de l'École*, n° 24, Paris, juillet 1978, p. 22-24.

Lacan, J. (1975b). Conférences et entretiens dans des universités nord-américaines In *Scilicet 6/7*, Paris: Seuil, 1976

Interpretation: From the Logic of the Signifier To the Po-et(h)ics of the Act

Ana Laura Prates

In a lecture from May 17th, 1977 Lacan puts forth the question: Is the psychoanalyst enough of a poet? Thus Lacan provokes us in Seminar 24 *L'insu que sait de l'une bévue s'aile à mourre* (1976-1977), stating that "only poetry allows for some interpretation." The connection of interpretation and poetry, and from there to the laws of language, is not exactly new in the teachings of Lacan. From the beginning he demonstrated – with Freud – that the symptom, as the dream, is a cipher whose logic responds to the same laws that rule over signifier combinations: metaphor and metonymy. ("Instance of the Letter"[33]: "the metaphoric structure, [...] indicates that the substitution of a signifier by a signifier brings about an effect of meaning, which is poetry or creation, p. 519).

This is, by principle, a statement of position: the Lacanian orientation as to the issue of interpretation in psychoanalysis. Now, it would not be excessive to affirm that interpretation, as the psychoanalyst's response, establishes the specificity of his discourse. If favorable, transference allows the psychoanalyst to interfere, with his act, in the analysand's work, that is, in free association.

But what would be the goal of this specific response that turns the discourse around, founding a new reason? As we said before,

---

[33] Jacques Lacan, "The Instance of the Letter in the Unconscious, or Reason Since Freud," *Ecrits*, W.W. Norton, 1966.

there are two overlapping aspects: the issue of truth and the issue of meaning.

We know that Freud was initially interested in interpretation in terms of exegesis: "What is this trying to say?" Taking *Interpretation of Dreams* (*Die Traumdeutung*) as paradigmatic of the psychoanalytic method, he intended to elucidate the hidden meanings of a dream by taking it as a text. Despite the fact that this meaning was a tributary of the subject's personal story, this did not nullify a certain initial kinship between psychoanalysis and hermeneutics, which still confuses the most unwary.

However, Freud soon realizes that the processes through which latent thoughts produce the manifest content of dreams – that is, condensation and displacement – are the same ones that produce the other formations of the unconscious: slips, jokes, and symptoms. Here, the shift from the hermeneutic to the structural plane is clear, since it is no longer possible to have the ordered pair of interpreter and interpreted, object and representation.

Thus, Freud soon realizes that, contrary to trying to exhaust the ultimate meaning of a dream – walking every path and deciphering each element to find, after close analysis, the final synthesis that would point at "the meaning" –, the analyst must rather enable the royal road of the unconscious, free association (Lacan called it signifier chain), to remain uninterrupted. In this way, interpretation – as Lacan will formalize in his text "The Direction of the Cure and the Principles of its Power" – is not merely a method to reach the repressed truth, nor is it a deciphering technique, but a piece of tactics relative to politics. We will return to this point later.

On the other hand, we cannot disregard Freud's turnings and re-turnings to the relationship between interpretation and the plane of reality. Despite the fact that dreams and symptoms are the realization of repressed infantile sexual desires, that is, they reveal the unconscious fantasy, Freud – and Frege, as we will see later – finds himself constantly limited by the question of reference to reality (as in the case of the Wolf Man, for example). This caused many problems for post-Freudian psychoanalysts. They lacked the concept of Real.

Let us move on to Lacan in 1972, to highlight this essential point: "[I]t is in the discourse on which the reality of fantasy is based that the real is inscribed."[34] From 1920 onwards, Freud wonders in an increasingly astute way about the limits of interpretation. In his homonymous text, "The Limits of Interpretation of Dreams" (1925), he points out the incomplete nature of interpretation, and in many cases, the impossibility of decision before the multiplicity of meanings.

Thus, what cannot be known and cannot be reached by recollection points towards repetition, the "pregnant drive," unreached by interpretation. To Freud, if the target of interpretation is secondary repression, then primary repression – constituent of the unconscious – can only be constructed. In the limits of recollection – alleged by interpretation – a direction for the treatment is found, which leads to the construction of fantasy. We say, with Lacan, where Freud splits away from the real, he places the reality of fantasy. This is another way to say that Freudian analysis concludes with the construction of fantasy, crashing against the rock of castration.

We know that Lacan's greatest merit during his "return to Freud" was precisely pointing out the structure of language of that rock, removed from the biologistic bias indicated by the "Oedipus

---

[34] El Aturdicho, *Otros escritos*, p. 478

Complex" and reissued in the person of the analyst under transference, as the pole of attraction of every interpretation in psychoanalysis. Hence all the deviations, as Lacan tired of denouncing, of a psychoanalytic clinic based on the interpretation of transference. Such an interpretation can only lead to an *acting-out*, as shown in the paradigmatic example of the case of Ernst Kris who, on his way out of the session, went to eat fresh monkey brains, after the analyst contrasted reality with his fantasy of being a plagiarist.

If we take the text "The Direction of The Cure and the Principles of its Power" as a parameter, we notice that at that moment Lacan displaces the question of reality (intended by post-Freudian interpretation) towards the question of truth, or in his own words: "The importance of the signifier in locating analytic truth." Here I would like to point out briefly that it is not about the idea of "true word" or "full speech" previously defined by Lacan, based on the notion of intersubjectivity and, therefore, intended to grasp the subject. As Lacan says: "No indicator is enough to show where the interpretation acts, if we do not radically accept some concept of the function of the signifier that captures the place where the subject subordinates himself to it, to the point of being subordinated by it" (*Escritos*, p. 599).

Truth as revealed by decryption, therefore, is not so much at the semantic level that would answer to "what is it that this means" as in the structure of "how does it say." Indeed, the Lacanian proposal of the 1950s to "take desire to the letter" indicates the extraction of fantasy via the logical structure of the signifier. Thus we can affirm that the response to the interpretation of desire is the fundamental fantasy, initially as a grammatical montage ("A Child is Being

Beaten," 1919) and later, in "Subversion of the Subject and the Dialectic of Desire" as "drive montage."

With the creation of the *object a* as remainder of the signifying operation of the causation of the subject, outside the chain but of the field of language, Lacan finally inaugurates a project that "makes School." Now, what the neurotic creates in his fantasy is an Other who demands his castration, or if he places him as an object, promotes his "de-subject-ification" and the annulment of his desire. Starting from the formulation of anguish as a median affect between *jouissance* and desire, an affect that is not deceptive and is produced by the "lack of the lack," Lacan promotes a clinical reformulation that allows one to think of it not only in terms of lack but fundamentally in terms of excess, since the *object a,* "cause of desire," is a creation of the subject's made positive in fantasy.

What are the consequences of this Lacanian turn towards interpretation? The first of them, obviously, is that interpretation must claim said cause of desire. This does not mean, as C. Soler (1994) warns us, that the object of fantasy must be targeted under penalty of making it consist even more. It is rather about the extraction of a piece of logic: "Interpretation does not claim the meaning but aims at reducing signifiers to their nonsense, so that we may rediscover the determinants of the whole behavior of the subject."[35]

The second consequence is a tributary of the debate with Laplanche, who had broken with Lacan, attributing the primacy of the unconscious in relation to language. Laplanche reduces the Lacanian proposal that interpretation must aim at the signifier as an

---

[35] Lacan, J. The four Fundamental Concepts of Psychoanalysis, 1973, Norton p. 201

authorization for infinite polysemy: interpretation would be open to any meaning. Lacan's proposal in Seminar 11 is forceful. He says: "Interpretation is not open to any meaning [...]. Interpretation is a signification that is not just any signification. It comes here in the place of the *s*, and reverses the relation by which the signifier has the effect, in language, of the signified. [Interpretation] has the effect of giving rise to an irreducible signifier."[36]

Here we see the writing of the analyst's discourse, as Lacan presented it in Seminar 17 *The Other Side of Psychoanalysis*, anticipated in an extraordinary way with the production of the S_1. In the same way, Lacan arrives at an *impasse* that we can call "impasse of fantasy,"[37] which is clearly expressed in Seminar 15 *The Analytic Act*. If fantasy, now formalized as "the writing of the impossible," is reduced to its logical operation, it paradoxically realizes that which has acquired truth value for the subject and, being constructed and traversed, it reveals that lack is pure loss. However, how is one to go beyond fantasy? The Lacanian clinic, conceived as "beyond the rock of castration," logically leads to the *impasse* of fantasy.

The idea that the analytic act is able to promote the traversal of the impasses of fantasy to the pass finds its institutional counterpart in the proposition of the pass as a *dispositif* capable of gathering the singularity of a passage that is not experienced merely at the level of the signifier. The imposition of formalizing this something, while not in the realm of language but in that of structure, leads Lacan to the writing of the four discourses as treatments of the impossible in the social bond. The fact that the "speechless – or wordless –

---

[36] Lacan, J. The four Fundamental Concepts of Psychoanalysis, Norton Press, p 250

[37] See Ronaldo Torres' book, *Dimensões do ato em psicanálise*.

discourses" are of the order of writing is something noteworthy, though we cannot develop it now.

To formalize the traversing of the *impasse* towards the pass, via the analytic act, Lacan, from my point of view, turns to two resources:

1. The creation of a subversion in the field of logic: the matheme that corresponds to the interpretation as apophantic (as explicitly proposed in the text *L'Étourdit* of 1972, contemporary to Seminar 20, *Encore*), and
2. The valuation of the act and, therefore, the development of the field of ethics: the po(ethics) [or the poem – or the *poâte*] that corresponds to interpretation as equivocal.[38]

"That it be said remains forgotten behind what is said in what is heard."[39] Here is the phrase that guides *L'Étourdit* and presents the radical thesis: what is said is not of the same order as saying. Lacan, who at various times had employed the terms 'meaning' and 'sense' in a somewhat confusing way, seems to take up again the distinction proposed by Frege in the text "Sense and Reference."[40] Frege, creator of Logicism, is interested in the relationship between language and reality. "To that end he establishes a fundamental and very influential distinction in the development of this debate between *Sinn* (sense) and *Bedeutung* (reference)" in which the first is related to connotation and the second to denotation (Marcondes,

---

[38] There is a brilliant text by C. Soler ("The Analyst's Responses"), of 1994, where she comments on *L'Étourdit*. I refer you to this text because we will not go into this exhaustively here. I also refer you to Christian Dunker's book, "Lacan and The Clinic of Interpretation" (1996), especially the chapter "The Logic of Interpretation"# which also contains comments on *L'Étourdit*. There are some points, however, that deserve comment to our purpose.

[39] Lacan, J. Outros Escritos, 2017

[40] N.T. Original German: *Über Sinn und Bedeutung*

D. p. 80). Frege further proposes a distinction between the logical form of a proposition and its grammatical form. His indication that the reference of a proposition is its truth value is quite consistent with Lacan's position on the logic of fantasy.

In *L'Étourdit* we find a rather peculiar articulation between modal logic and propositional logic which for Frege would be unacceptable, since its prerogative is that propositions of the indicative type can be true or false and thus they are the only ones to have a reference. Modal logic uses exactly the modalities that indicate possibilities such as 'necessary,' 'possible,' 'contingent' and 'impossible.' Lacan affirms that the first phrase "that it be said" – which points at the saying, because it is in the subjunctive grammatical mode – falls on the modal side. Thus he concludes something extraordinary: the saying ex-sists to the truth,[41] since the attribution of falsity or truth would not apply to it. Now, if the propositional affirmation is in the field of sayings, we must consider nonetheless that "for a said thing to be true, a saying is still necessary."[42]

The complexity of what Lacan articulates here is extraordinary. We could be tempted to place on the one side the propositional function and the meaning/reference (*Bedeutung*) of the phallus and, on the other, the modal, on the side of "a saying" that acquires meaning from the place of the *semblant* it occupies. What Lacan is formalizing, however, is more complex, since "what is said goes not without saying."[43] So, it is necessary for the saying to take the place of a master signifier so that the sayings may articulate with the truth,

---

[41] Lacan, J. Outros Escritos, 2017, p.449; translated by A.Z.
[42] Ibid.; translated by A.Z.
[43] Ibid., p. 451; translated by A.Z.

albeit fantastic. Thus the saying is manifested by escaping what is said, and it ex-sists in relation to truth. Interpretation is sense, according to Lacan, and it goes against meaning.[44]

This is a dramatic turn in Lacan regarding the relationship between truth and the real. Let's see what Lacan says to this respect in Seminar 23:

Remembering consists of making these chains go into something that is already there and is referred to as knowledge; (...) what Freud holds as unconscious always supposes a piece of knowledge, and a spoken knowledge at that. The unconscious is entirely reducible to a certain knowledge. It is the minimal thing that supposes the fact that it may be interpreted. Clearly this knowing demands at least two supports, which we call terms, symbolizing them by letters. Hence my writing of knowledge as supported by S with index S_2. I define the signifier, to which I confer the support S index 1, as that which represents a subject as such and represents it truly. *Truly* means, in this case, *according to reality*. True, that is, conforming to reality. Reality, in this case, is what truly functions. But what functions truly has nothing to do with what I designate as real. (...) In other words, the instance of knowledge as renewed by Freud, I mean renewed under the form of the unconscious, does not necessarily presuppose in any way the real I make use of" (Lacan, "Joyce – The Symptom," p. 127/128).

The real, that is to say, the impossible character of the sexual relationship, is what commands truth. Thus the phallic function replaces the sexual relationship; the subject, as the pure effect of meaning, is "a response of the real."[45] And this is why Lacan holds

---

[44] Ibid., p. 481; translated by A.Z.
[45] Lacan, J. Outros Escritos, 2017, p. 458; translated by A.Z.

that it is only in the analytic discourse that "saying" ex-sists, since it is thanks to interpretation that the analyst is able, with his specific saying, to operate on the modal content of the neurotic demand that envelops the whole of the sayings, thus extracting a saying.

Note that Lacan introduces yet another problem here, specifying precisely that the modal saying falls on the side of demand, that is, on the side of neurosis. Neurosis suspends the affirmation via the infinite suspension of the decision: "it could be this" or "it could be that." In this way the subject does not need to position himself. The analyst's saying, on the contrary, is of the order of the apophantic. Now, traditionally, the apophantic has been applied since Aristotle to the propositional, that is, to the statements to which truth value may be attributed. In other words, how should something that seems to "say about" be applied, according to Lacan, to the order of what is said? How is something of the order of truth to be attributed to the analyst's saying?

I think it is necessary to take the etymology of the word apophantic: apo (away from) and phaos (light[46]). The apophantic, thus, aims at something of the order of illumination, a revelation. It is curious that Lacan, after affirming that the saying of interpretation has an apophantic status, returns to the fact that interpretation has bearing on the cause of desire. He adds: "a cause which [interpretation] reveals." Later, he affirms that "structure is the real that comes to light in language." So, I think the term apophantic is not so much an attribution of truth to the saying of the analyst, but rather something that aims at, that illuminates, the limit of truth, that is, the real.

---

[46] T.N. Original *luz* means light as in sunlight. It is unrelated to weight unlike its term in English.

If Lacan is saying that the master's discourse, that of the unconscious and which "founds the reality of fantasy"[47] and establishes the structure, inscribes a saying and makes contingency necessary, then the practice of the analyst "must procure such cuts in the discourse that modify its original structure."[48]

This is how Lacan subverts Aristotle's propositional logic with Frege, introducing an unthinkable mode for any consistent logic: "The saying of analysis realizes the apophantic which by its simple ex-sistence is distinguished from proposition."[49] Thus he puts the propositional function in its place, "since it provides us with the only support that makes up for the ab-sense (absence/non-sense) of the sexual relationship."[50]

And here we enter the last point of my development that I have named poetics of the act, and that, it seems to me, Lacan emphasizes at the end of that text, continuing the theme in the late Seminars of his teachings. What is the analyst's weapon against the reductive modes of the neurotic demand? I say reductive because Lacan teaches that the demand reduces the impossible into the contingent, and the possible into the necessary. Again we see the exclusion of the real as impossible, typical of neurosis. The analyst with his act "operates with the equivocation by which each *lalangue* is distinguished."[51]

One of the most beautiful phrases from *L'Étourdit*: "A language among others is nothing more than the integral of misunderstandings that its history has allowed to persist. It is the

---

[47] Lacan, J. Étourdit 478
[48] Ibid. 479
[49] Ibid. 492
[50] Ibid.
[51] Ibid.

stratum in which the real – the one thing, according to the analytic discourse, to motivate its result, the real that there is no sexual relationship – was deposited throughout the ages."[52]

As to interpretation by equivocation, Lacan privileges homophony, the plays and puns of language that, according to him, are the ones that play us, except for "when the poets calculate them and the psychoanalyst makes uses of them when convenient."[53] To homophony we could also add homonymy and that inter-language play the paradigm of which is Joyce's text.

We frequently hear that Joyce's text does not make sense. Perhaps we could correct this statement saying that, if we stick to semantics, it may fail to signify. Regarding meaning, we find such a great proliferation that it loses value (remember the truth value of fantasy), thus leaning towards the ab-sense. Each phrase in Joyce was built like a sculpture, in a completely artificial and calculated way. It is not automatic writing. Lacan, I think, makes of this a sort of methodological paradigm.

We find this method, for example, in the very title of Seminar 24: *L'Insue que sait de l'une bévue s'aille a mourre*. From the standpoint of a semantic translation, we get: The not-known that knows about an equivocal goes to hell."[54] By way of equivocation we get: love, to the wall, to death. Or: failure, the unconscious. Or, on the side of the verb: knows, is. And so on. Thus, I think Lacan is proposing, in a (po)ethical act, the "monstration" (beyond demonstration) of what he has referred to in Seminar 23: using equivocation until spent. Let us not forget that while in the topology

---

[52] Ibid.

[53] Ibid., 493.

[54] Hand game that consists of matching the number of fingers shown between two players, a.k.a. *jankenpon, cachipún* or rock-paper-sissors.

of *L'Etourdit* meaning seems to be at times between the symbolic and the real, in the Borromean knot, meaning is in the knotting of the imaginary and the symbolic, since the real ex-sists to the meaning. Use it until spent: here is the lie, the trick of the psychoanalyst. I think Lacan uses the rings of string (*ronds de ficelles*), which also means "trick" in French, precisely to realize the "monstration" of the impossibility of displacing the weight of the meaning towards "the weight of the real" without the "sediments of language."

In the conference given in Brussels on February 26, 1977, Lacan affirms that psychoanalysis has no exit other than passing through meaning and, necessarily, through words. Lacan says that Freud arrives at this in his *Studies in Hysteria*: "(...) it is with words that this is solved and it is with the patient's own words that the affect evaporates."[55]

For Lacan, therefore, it is about giving the unconscious another body, different from the idea of representation: "the unconscious." Words are enough there; words make body, and this does not mean that anything is understood at all. That is the unconscious: one is guided by words of which nothing is understood. What lies outside, therefore, is the weight of meaning. In its place, Lacan puts the weight of the real.

The question that is never silent is what is the relationship of language with the real. Lacan responds to it in quite a direct way: "The essence of what Freud said is that there is the greatest relationship between this use of words in a species that has words at

---

[55] Sigmund Freud, Studies in Hysteria (1893-1895), in The Standard Edition of the Complete Psychological Works of Sigmund Freud, Vol. II, trans. James Strachey (London: Hogarth Press, 1971), 108.

its disposal, and the sexuality that rules over said species."[56] "Sexuality is completely enveloped in words, this is the essential step that he took. It is much more important than knowing what they mean."[57] This is the essential clinical question: interpretation does not aim at "what does it mean," but at the fact of "it being said."

Translation: Andrea Zorzutti

---

[56] Jacques Lacan, Seminar XXIII: The Sinthome, trans. by A. R. Price (Polity, 2016)

[57] Jacques Lacan, *Seminar XXIII: The Sinthome*, trans. by A. R. Price (Polity, 2016)

Something Borrowed, Something New...

Matías Laje

– We can't change the country.
Let us change the subject.
James Joyce, *Ulysses.*

It happened in the early days of psychoanalysis when, in Vienna, Theodor Reik was accused of quackery. This serious, overt allegation against a close disciple of Freud was indeed a stroke aimed at psychoanalytic practice itself. Freud not only took an open stance on behalf of his friend, but also seized an opportunity to publish, as a sort of disclaimer, a manifesto for training analysis as it was then called. I'm certainly referring to *The Question of Lay Analysis*.[58] The true Freudian concern in the article is what can and cannot be expected from an analyst. While undergoing an analytic cure is a logical and ethical part of the practice of psychoanalysis, whether one is a physician or not is unimportant. In the premise of the accusation against Reik, there is a relevant question to a school of psychoanalysis. It's not easy to find a way to determine if someone is practicing psychoanalysis, and not something else. Nonetheless, at least in a Lacanian perspective, it is never about who is allowed to perform psychoanalysis. It's about clarifying what happened when a psychoanalysis worked out well.

The second part of the title, *Conversations with an Impartial Person,* refers to the interview-like arrangement of the article and it

---

[58] Sigmund Freud, *The Question of Lay Analysis: Covers* (New York: W. W. Norton & Company, 1990).

also features a key aspect in every analytic session – a conversation with an *impartial* person. Free association has a lot to do with impartiality, yet it's not a call for purity. *Le désir de l'analyste n'est pas un désir pur*[59]... Lacan said, right after his excommunication from the IPA. We can expect from an analyst a certain craft as a listener, for sure, and that has also something to do with free association.

The Freudian notion of *freien Einfällen*[60], as established in *Traumdeutung*, is perhaps what is usually translated as "free associations." *Einfall* is an idea or remark as it occurs, which may happen to be a proper formation of the unconscious in analysis. So, *free*... from what? There is an important difference to make here. Free association is not a psychological, cognitive, or linguistic phenomenon or type of relation – it's the experience of the unconscious in analytic discourse. Therefore, free association is not free in the sense of something pure. Why? Because in analysis, the formations of the unconscious depend upon the position of the analyst, toward which the unconscious is directed. The analyst is required but can also spoil the chance. Freud was aware of this and, concerning the use of dreams in analysis, developed a method in order to prevent "wild interpretations" [*verwilderten Deutunge*],[61] which were in fashion from ancient times up to his own in the 1900s. Freud proposes to let the dreamer be the interpreter, even if the dreamer is not aware of it. However, the impartiality Freud required from the analyst as a condition for analytic, hence subjective, interpretation is attained through a great deal of activity.

---

[59] Jacques Lacan, Seminar XI, *The Four Fundamental Concepts of Psychoanalysis*, (Paris: Seuil, 1973), 248.
[60] Sigmund Freud, *Traumdeutung* (London: Imago Publishing Co., 1942), 358.
[61] Idem.

If the output comes under the form of silence, it's a desire-driven silence, making room for the unconscious to occur. Nevertheless, what Lacan named in 1967 as *destitution subjective*[62] is not just sitting in the office in front of a stranger, waiting for something to happen. Even as the analyst utters a verbal interpretation (given that it later turns out to be one), their subjectivity remains actively silent. Maybe these conditions are necessary to experience free association in analytic discourse. Still, what is its aim? This is an ethical question.

In order to give an answer, I will use the concept of the unconscious Lacan put forward in "The Function and Field of Speech and Language in Psychoanalysis"[63] and Position of the Unconscious.[64] By *concept* I don't mean just a definition of the unconscious, but also its domain in practice. One may ask if nowadays its position remains the same. As far as I can tell, something hasn't changed since *Fonction et champ...*, when Lacan called the unconscious a *transindividual*[65] experience. Later on, the precision tool of *Position of the Unconscious* located the unconscious between the subject and the Other, *coupure en acte*[66], cut in act. Interpretation is certainly a cutting act. It's a strong definition and it doesn't apply to all interpretations, yet it does to some, when there's an effect of no return in the analysand. So, back

---

[62] Jacques Lacan, "Proposition sur le psychanalyste de l'École," in *Autres écrits* (Paris: Éditions du Seuil, 2001), 252.

[63] Jacques Lacan, "The Function and Field of Speech and Language in Psychonalysis," *Ecrits,* W.W. Norton, 1966.

[64] Jacques Lacan (1960)

[65] Jacques Lacan, "Fonction et champ de la parole et du langage en psychanalyse," in *Écrits I* (Paris: Éditions du Seuil, 1970), 136.

[66] Jacques Lacan, "Position de l'inconscient," in *Écrits II* (Paris: Éditions du Seuil, 1971), 205.

to its aims... The value of the unconscious in analysis does not come from the sheer love for truth, nor the scientific requirements for anamnesis. What the unconscious brings to analysis, and especially to the symptom of the subject, comes through by means of interpretation. Is it just about knowing a bit more about that odd part of yourself? That can be a bait in the beginning, but that's not it. The desire of the analyst allows both the analyst and the analysand to surpass the need for knowledge.

When someone is so delicate or urged to bring a dream to analysis, it is more than just a chance to solve a puzzle. The significance of Freud's *Traumdeutung* is to seize that dream, to use what comes out of it, as an interpretation of the position of the dreamer at an ethical crossroads regarding desire. What is the *scene* the dream has come to tell in a way the analysand's ego would never be able to formulate, pressed as it is by sense, prejudice and ideology? Beware! Free association comes not only to be read, but to change the position of the subject. This seldom happens, but when it does, *la passe*.... Free association is not always welcomed by the patient, especially at the beginning of analysis. If uncanny at first, it can become delightfully surprising. There is certainly an act in letting someone else be the subject in analysis. This implies something different than just authorizing oneself to receive patients.

So now we've come to another very important question for a School of Psychoanalysis: can free association happen outside the analytic session? Or, perhaps, I could ask this in another way: What is the extensive rapport of the School to the unconscious? I'm not talking about the obvious, which is sometimes interesting as well, in the sense of saying out loud whatever comes to your mind in a School meeting or cartel. I think that there is a true bond to the unconscious in a cartel when it leads – as it sometimes does – to a different transindividual and pulsatile experience of the desire of the analyst in the School. Many times I get *less* tired after working in a cartel.

I guess free association may have a special resonance in the "Land of the Free," where Theodor Reik developed his practice. So, I want to make it clear. Free association is not "free" as unbound, nor costless. Absolute freedom has a very high price regarding social bond and it logically leads to a-social bondage. James Joyce is an example of someone who took from *lalanglaise* something to change literature as we know it, and being a *lord of language* wasn't costless at all for him. Didn't Lacan himself expand the Freudian experience, in a way that analysis and what came next was never the same after his *hérésie*? I wish for, in a Lacanian inspiration, a use of free association to reveal the signifier, to touch the subject of language, and to produce a hole through which something new can happen in analysis. *Parlêtre*[67] may be the name of that outcome, very much like the way that work-in-progress, *James Joyce*, is not so different from the result of an analysis. It is remarkable what Joyce did without free association, though at first this may seem hard to grasp due to the formal pirouettes of his verbal jouissance. So, what matters is not only free association in analysis, but the haptic use of interpretation in the cure, when it reaches the body through an analytic symptom.

Since the cause of desire is in the Other, the effects of analysis on the subject won't be brand new in the end, yet will be totally unknown until experienced. There are many who state that analysis has no ending, since there is no complete resolution to the

---

[67] Jacques Lacan, "Joyce le Symptôme," in *Autres écrits* (Paris: Éditions du Seuil, 2001), 565.

symptomatic satisfactions of the Freudian drive. Particularly within the School of Psychoanalysis of the Lacanian Field, as it is sometimes described in *Wunsch* magazine, it's not just the symptom but its rapport with the desire of the analyst that can be the proof of the end. By means of something borrowed from the analyst, the *parlêtre* reaches a new position, freer in a way, yet not absolutely free from the Other.

Bibliography

Freud, Sigmund. *The Question of Lay Analysis.* New York: W. W. Norton & Company, 1990.

Freud, Sigmund. *Traumdeutung.* London: Imago Publishing Co., 1942.

Joyce, James. *Ulysses.* London: Penguin Books, 2000.

Lacan, Jacques. "Fonction et champ de la parole et du langage en psychanalyse," in *Écrits I,* 111-208. Paris: Éditions du Seuil, 1970.

Lacan, Jacques. "Position de l'inconscient," in *Écrits II,* 193-217. Paris: Éditions du Seuil, 1971.

Lacan, Jacques. *Le Séminaire*, Livre XI, *Les quatre concepts fondamentaux de la psychanalyse.* Paris: Éditions du Seuil, 1973.

Lacan, Jacques. "Proposition sur le psychanalyste de l'École," in *Autres écrits,* 243-259. Paris: Éditions du Seuil, 2001.

Lacan, Jacques. "Joyce le Symptôme," in *Autres écrits,* 565-573. Paris: Éditions du Seuil, 2001.

The Structure of the Cartel as Structure and Engineering in the School: From the Gateway to the Pass, the Cartel

Sonia Alberti

I

All of us, when we arrive at the Lacanian School, are faced with this door that reads "Cartel." The Cartel is the gateway to the School, in such a way Plato posted the saying: "Let none but geometers enter here" at the gateway of the Academia (cf. Lacan, 1966-67, session of April, 12). And when you enter a Cartel (the best thing you can do when entering the School), it has to do with the desire to know. The way this knowledge will take place depends on whether the Cartel will actually work or not. This is because its structure, as Lacan proposed, especially in its refined formula, implies the transfer of work with the text that is studied in it. This asks the *cartelisant* to position himself as a subject in the hysterical discourse, that is, the place of the subject who questions the established knowledge – the S1. The hysteric subject can do this because he/she sustains him/herself by what causes him/her. In this context, what causes him to work in a Cartel is precisely something that the known knowledge does not know. The Cartel, in order to function, requires that any and all *cartelants* bring something of their own subject causality, and that reveals the Other's hole. This is, in fact, the best, the only way to truly learn.

It is quite interesting to investigate it in light of what Lacan comments in his first seminar when referring to the teaching of Buddhist monks.[68]

The master breaks the silence with anything – with a sarcastic remark, with a kick-start.

That is how a Buddhist master conducts his search for meaning, according to the technique of Zen. It behooves the students to find out for themselves the answer to their own questions. The master does not teach *ex cathedra* a ready-made science; he supplies an answer when the students are on the verge of finding it.

This kind of teaching is a refusal of any system. It uncovers a thought in motion–nonetheless vulnerable to systematization, since it necessarily possesses a dogmatic aspect. Freud's thought is the most perennially open to revision. It is a mistake to reduce it to a collection of hackneyed phrases. Each of his ideas possesses a vitality of its own. That is precisely what one calls the dialectic.

Certain of these ideas were, at a given moment, indispensable to Freud, because they supplied an answer to a question that he had formulated previously, in other terms. Hence one only gains a sense of their value by relocating them in their context.

But it is not enough to do some history, the history of thought, and to say that Freud lived in a scientific century. Rather, with *The Interpretation of Dreams*, something of a different essence, of a concrete psychological density, is reintroduced, namely, meaning.

From the scientific point of view, Freud appeared at this point to revert to the most archaic thinking–reading something in dreams. He alters returns to causal explanations. But when one interprets a

---

[68]Jacques Lacan, *Seminar I: Freud's Papers on Technique*, trans. John Forrester, ed. Jacques-Alain Miller (New York: Norton, 1991), 1.

dream, one is always up to one's neck in meaning. What is at issue is the subjectivity of the subject, in his desires, in his relation to his environment, to others, to life itself.

Our task, here, is to reintroduce the register of meaning, a register that must itself be reintegrated on its own level.

Despite this, the working through in the Cartel is identified by Lacan as a transference in work [*transfert de travail*] – opposed to a psychoanalysis which he identifies, with Freud, as a work of transference [*travail de transfert*]. This means that there is, of course, a reference to the established knowledge, but the position of the subject in the transference in work is quite different from the one in the Buddhist context. First of all, because the Cartel takes its sense from the fact that it is located in an institution which with particularity is that of Lacan's School. It's a group, but inside a system whose only "dogma" is that there is no "dogma," the only rules are: there is an impossible to know, the subject is driven by the pleasure principle, the tendency towards low and homeostatic stimulus, as Lacan (1986) derives it from Freud, and its beyond: jouissance. In the same way that the structure of the subject organizes itself around the hole – the object is lost and the repression is original and indelible – the School is a collective formation organized around the absence of a pre-established concept of the analyst. The absence of a conclusive and total knowledge on this matter – what the analyst is – enables each one to elaborate a personal answer for his/her bond towards the School, taking into account his/her desire and relation with the analytic cause.

This takes me to the question I raise here today, trying to build a link between the Cartel as the basis of the School and the Pass, where, betting on each other's analytical experience, the Cartels of the Pass try to decant something else about what the analyst is, knowing that the answers will never be conclusive nor total.

So, let's go back to the Cartel as an entrance to the School when there is a desire to know. Yes, *when,* since there may be other uses of joining a Cartel, for instance, to come together with other people – something these days we need very much in order not to succumb to the social isolation to which we are taken because of the pandemic, but which was already there before the pandemic for many people, driven by the capitalistic discourse which orients us against the social link... By the way, Lacan himself already observed that the School as a concept takes its origin from the school in ancient Greek history – a place where you may feel at home, amongst your friends or partners – which tells us that the use of a Cartel to be with others is not a bad idea...

But since the Cartel is said by the School to be its foundation, when we get in touch with the School, we are invited or even prompted by an appeal or demand which provokes a possible encounter towards elaboration. We elaborate from... are provoked by... we work in response to a provocation. And this has to do with the logic of the discourses which are, as Lacan defines them in his Seminar XVII (1969/70), bonds of jouissance: we position ourselves in a discourse to enjoy, even as the discourse produces jouissance.[69]

The discourse we could develop from the observation mentioned above, on the relation between a Buddhist teacher and his students, is the one Lacan calls the master's discourse:

$$\frac{S_1}{\$} \longrightarrow \frac{S_2}{a}$$

---

[69] Jacques Lacan, *Seminar XVII: The Other Side of Psychoanalysis*, trans. Russell Grigg, ed. Jacques-Alain Miller (New York: Norton, 2007).

The master puts his students to work – he provokes them with his kick – and what they elaborate is the product of this action, but eventually, it's only garbage, the object *a*, to be put into the trash because of the necessary dogmatic aspect pinpointed by Lacan in the above-cited passage. What the subject – the students – produce is just a +value in that dogmatic system. Therefore they can be represented by the S2, the way Lacan associates it with Meno, Plato's slave...[70]

But, in *Television*,[71] Lacan (1974) observes that the psychoanalyst provokes something different: the turning of the discourses. When Lacan observes in his very first Seminar that our task, as psychoanalysts, is to reintroduce the subjectivity of the subject, this is already the turning of the discourses: from the master's discourse, to the hysterical one, which gives us the reference to articulate the work in the Cartel of the Lacanian School.

$$\frac{\$}{\_a} \dashrightarrow \frac{\_S_1}{S_2}$$

Being in a transference of work (transfert de travail) to the collectivity of the School – and this is why a Cartel is registered in the School – a subject puts his questions to the established knowledge, the texts the Cartel is studying, in order to put this knowledge – the master's knowledge – to work, and elaborate it with the others in the Cartel. This may produce new knowledge. Lacan calls the S_2 knowledge itself since a signifier never means something in itself. It's when a subject chooses a book from a shelf and reads it that the book becomes alive. Alone on the shelf it doesn't mean

---

[70] *Ibid*, pg. 22.Sem. 17, session of November, 26.
[71] Lacan, J. Television, 1990). Television (1974). New York/London, Norton & Company. Translated by Denis Hollier, Rosalind Krauss, and Annette Michelson.

anything, only that there is a book. The subject ($) that brings this book (S_2) to life, does so supported by his singular reference, which is under the bar on his side: the object (*a*) that causes him/her to ask the S_1. S_2 is the produced knowledge. That is the hysteric model of the discourses.

The work in a Cartel determines the work of the School, from its outskirts to its very bone, the Pass. When I say outskirts, I want to denote that it is possible to participate in a Cartel even if one is not a Forum or a School member, but this is already a way to experiment with the possibility of acting from the place where the subject is taken into account as someone who may contribute with something. In this way, due to its structure, the analytic discourse is the only one properly directed toward the subject:

$$\frac{a}{\underline{S_2}} \longrightarrow \frac{\$}{S_1}$$

The Cartel as the gateway determines the work of the School. Each one who participates in the School will do what he/she can and in his/her own way. I mean, each one will live this experience attributing his/her own meanings that will come from the experiences with the other participants of the Cartel itself and even of the School. These meanings are usually still associated with those that the cartelisant brings from his own history and from the marks of the relationships lived, which imply the social bonds with his others, not without reference to the Other of each one.

In the matheme of the hysteric discourse, the subject is located at the place of the agent, to question this known knowledge, and if this is the structure that best identifies the cartelisant in a true Cartel work, then it is necessary that those who meet in the transference of work, aiming to know, be subjects. A subject is one, in an articulation of RSI,[72] that when they are tied together, it includes the object *a*, the place where it is no longer a question of knowledge. On the contrary, it signals the impossible to know in this structure or, as said, what causes the desire to know at the gateway of the School.

In the same way that an analysis causes the subject to know the knowledge that he did not know, the Cartel also provokes the subject to know what is elaborated in that work when the questioning in the hysterical position of the known knowledge, in the texts, in the books – instruments of the Cartel's work – is confronted with the desire to know caused by the presence of the object *a* of the structure of the hysterical subject. It is quite usual that someone who works in a Cartel has or at least has had already some analytical experience. This means that he/she has already had the opportunity to meet with an analyst. The analyst, if he is really one, has taken this subject into account, and it is known that the analytic experience produces something Lacan called hysterization. Anyhow, we know that an analyst is the product of an analysis, and if any analysis is didactic, as Lacan uses it, then the subject who encountered an analyst will have experienced the jouissance of the hysterical discourse as the possibility for him to know. This was the title of Lacan's journal, *Scilicet* (1968...), a Greek word that means "thou mayst know" or "it is permitted thee to know," especially if you were not wed to a psychoanalytic society at those times.

Yes, only if you were not married to a psychoanalytic society – which in *Television,* Lacan calls the "Mutual Aid Society Against the Analytical Discourse" [SAMCDA – Societé d'Aide Mutuel Contre le Discours Analytique] – since in those times Lacan still

---

[72] RSI is in reference to Lacan's formulation of the Real, Symbolic and Imaginary.

struggled against the established discourse of the IPA, where every knowledge was taught to be predetermined. The agent of the hysterical discourse, on the contrary, because it is in fact supported by the object *a*, the cause of desire – even if he is still quite unaware of how much he, himself, is this object as well – opens new possible elaborations, which he will also gain through his own analysis when he will be confronted with the logic of his fantasy.

II

A second moment is illustrated by the function of + 1. If the place of the +1 is that of just one more member working in the Cartel, it is not without accumulating the function of what causes the Cartel to work and, in that, it is associated with the position of the object *a* which, in the hysteric's discourse, is under the bar, but in the Cartel, it needs to appear. The +1 also takes the position of the object to cause the work that is the elaboration the Cartel does to know and, therefore, dependent on the desire to know. From the place of the object, the +1 necessarily involves a subjective destitution and, if this does not occur, such as when the +1 identifies him/herself to the place of the master, or when he/she does not assume this role with the other cartelisants, remaining exclusively in the place of the subject, what we'll have is a frustrated Cartel, it won't happen. Because it is the function of the +1 to sustain the hole of knowing so that this can provoke the cartelisants to work. That is why we could call the object function of the +1 the −1 (minus one), the place of the hole.

To exercise it, we are no longer at the entrance door of the School, we have already entered it in some way. Even if we have not yet become members of the School, a +1 is, at the same time, a subject in the transference of work – since he is just +1 (plus one) subject in the Cartel – and he is also a −1, the object causing work.

He might be anyone, but has to be someone – says Lacan. But he will provoke the work of elaboration and I think that, if he really does it, somehow he must be able to assume this position of the –1, he needs to have this experience of this position, perhaps from others, already gained through previous Cartel experience, and a knowledge of the experience about the Cartel's place in the School. The Cartel, while it is a cheered reference in the School for representing a form of work that allows valuing the "thou mayst know" of each cartelisant, needs that this someone supports the –1 and only then the role of the Cartel in the School becomes clearer and clearer. As for the association with the analysis itself, the fact that the position of the –1 includes something of the subjective destitution demands that the someone has had an opportunity to have crossed something of the subjective destitution. This also implies having perceived something about how fantasy is constituted: on the one hand, the subject, on the other, the object, in the matheme that Lacan dedicated to fantasy, in which the subject is not only necessarily divided, but that he is also the object, called *a*, that which fell from the Other, from the fact that the Other is inconsistent.

Now, we know that the object *a* falls from the Other when the bar that castrates him strikes, and if in the hysteric's discourse we use the object *a* to question the master in the expectation that he can still show himself without fail – here, in the association with the Cartel, that the text still might explain why this, why that – , the +1 will use it in the opposite way: he/she uses the object *a* to make the discourses rotate, valuing what each Cartel-subject's contribution is worth – including his own – since Lacan proposed that the product of the work was to be not collective but to be the product of each one. Each one can contribute to the knowledge that is elaborated there, depending on what leads these subjects to do a Cartel, the desire to know.

In previous texts I and my co-authors propose that the +1 assumes this position of the object *a* in the hysteric discourse at the moment when the object *a* is no longer under the bar but visible. And the matheme for it, instead of:

$$\frac{\$}{a} \longrightarrow \frac{S_1}{S_2}$$

would be:

$$a \longrightarrow \$ \longrightarrow \frac{S_1}{S_2}$$

It describes it as the *ascesis* of the +1. An *ascesis* is defined as the practice of severe self-discipline, typically for religious reasons. But we could try to follow this in another direction, which I am trying to pinpoint: in the direction of the awareness of the two terms of the fantasy, which means that the function of the +1 may contribute to the elaboration of both, the position that a subject assumes as subject but also that of the object which, in this case, puts the subject to work.

III

In his Seminar in the years 1976-77, on the L'*Insu*, Lacan demonstrates how desire has a meaning, in the same way as he once identified the full speech (parole pleine). In fact, he criticizes what he presented in "Function and Field of Speech and Language," when there he contrasted *full* with *empty* speech, privileging the first over the second. *Full speech*, he says in 1977, is full of meaning, whereas empty speech has only signification.

This Seminar was given years after his Third Speech in Rome (1974), where Lacan was very much preoccupied with the filling with meaning in the practice of psychoanalysis. In this text, he observes that science and religion give sense all the time and that psychoanalysis is in danger if meaning prevails over the very hole of the Freudian cause. Filling it with meaning would only nourish true religion as well as the false one, while the psychoanalyst should be a symptom, an intrusion of the real.

And it is around this that I plan to weave with you the third moment, which I articulate here with the Pass.

From the entering in the School to the Pass, there is this elaboration which implies knowledge but always around the hole of the real, which the structure of the Cartel sustains. But since there is never an intention in the School to identify a finished formation – in psychoanalysis the formations are those of the unconscious – not even with the pass there is a full formation, the School is of continuous formation, and always, every day, each one is also at it's gateway, in the sense that each member of the School chooses every day to cross the entrance again.

That is why Lacan attributes, in this Seminar on the L'Insu, an emptiness to signification, in opposition to the full speech. In relation to the Cartel, in this context, we could say that a Cartel in Lacan's School is only a signifier that produces effects of signification, and that is why it works for the School of Lacan as its gateway. There are three moments, in Lacan's articulations, to think about the relationship between meaning and signification.

In the first moment of his teaching, Lacan bets on the meaning. We read it in his first words from *Seminar I: Freud's Papers on Technique*. Let's see the presentation of the first lesson of his first published seminar, what does he say there? Something very similar to what I was pointing out in relation to the functioning of the Cartel at the first moment of the Cartel making sense at the entrance to the School. "Our task, here, is to reintroduce the register of meaning, a register that must itself be reintegrated on its own level."[73] In "Function and Field of Speech and Language," it is still in the search for the meaning of Freud's discovery that Lacan[74] insists, when he mentions the important task of freeing psychoanalysis, as it was practiced in 1953, of the notions that were amortized in a routine use of technical rules: "I consider it to be an urgent task to isolate, in concepts that are being deadened by routine use, the meaning they recover when we reexamine their history and reflect on their subjective foundations."[75]

But very quickly, already in Seminar 1, the meaning includes the non-sense, and as the seminar progresses, this is more and more what is interesting to Lacan: the non-sense, as well as the sense, of the Freudian discovery. In the same seminar, but almost at the end, Lacan mentions the signifier, in the context of resuming the analysis of dreams:

> He tells us about the *Tagesreste,* the day residues, which are, he says, disinvested from the point of view of desire. These are, within the dream, the stray forms which have become, for the subject, of minimal importance – and are emptied of their meaning. So this is a piece of signifying material. The signifying material, be it phonematic, hieroglyphic, etc., is constituted out of forms which have forfeited their own meaning and are taken

---

[73] Jacques Lacan, *Seminar I: Freud's Papers on Technique,* trans. John Forrester, ed. Jacques-Alain Miller (New York: Norton, 1991), pg. 245.

[74] Jacques Lacan, *Seminar V: Formations of the Unconscious,* trans by R. Grigg (Polity, 2017)
Formations of the unconscious

[75] Jacques Lacan, "The Function and Field of Speech and Language in Psychoanalysis," in *Écrits,* trans. Bruce Fink (New York: Norton, 2006).

up again within a new organisation [sic], thanks to which another meaning finds a means of gaining expression.[76]

As Lacan advances in the approach of what he calls at this time the "signifying material" (the material constituted by signifiers), and deepens his studies in the field of language – which he already privileges in this first published Seminar, and that he delves into deeper in "Function and Field…" – the richness, the complexity of the Freudian discovery of the function of the signifier gradually relativizes the function of sense. The meaning is now much more related to non-sense, associated with the metaphor: "We see that metaphor is situated at the precise point at which meaning is produced in nonmeaning"[77] (as exemplified with the sentence, "Love is a pebble laughing in the sun,"[78] a non-sense sentence, a metaphor which, therefore gives it a whole signification, because it "recreates love in a dimension that I have said strikes me").[79]

In "The Agency of the Letter in the Unconscious or Reason Since Freud,"[80] Lacan observes:

"From where it can be said that it is in the signifying chain where the sense *insists,* but that none of the elements of the chain *consist* in the signification of which it is capable in that very moment. The notion of an incessant sliding of meaning under the signifier is thus imposed."[81] This sentence comes in handy here for us, because we find in it the three terms together: the meaning that

---

[76] Jacques Lacan, *Seminar I: Freud's Papers on Technique,* trans. John Forrester, ed. Jacques-Alain Miller (New York: Norton, 1991), pg 245.

[77] Jacques Lacan, "The Instance of the Letter in the Unconscious or Reason Since Freud," in *Écrits, a Selection,* trans. Alan Sheridan (New York: Norton, 1977).

[78] ibid op cit

[79] ibid op cit

[80] ibid op cit

[81] ibid op cit page 153

insists, the signification that consists, and the signifier that imposes itself.

As the signifier imposes itself in Lacan's teaching as a determinant in conjunction with another signifier, the sense is increasingly articulated with what is of the order of the imaginary, of the feeling, and, with the equivocacy so perfect in the French language, in which the word *sentiment*, for feeling, is also the sense that lies, *ment*. On the other hand, the truth that would be associated with the full speech, charged with meaning, empties itself more and more as articulated to what was initially alluded to with the non-sense, to then articulate it with castration.

With the "Signification of the Phallus," from 1958, this settles down, but only there where the paternal metaphor signs in, since "From this "why," correlatively, the significance of castration in fact takes on its (clinically manifest) full weight as far as the formation of symptoms is concerned, only on the basis of its discovery as castration of the mother."[82]

This is where signification and meaning distance themselves, inexorably, in Lacan's teaching, and the association of signifiers takes place in the field of the symbolic, which necessarily always creates a real, because when you affirm something in the symbolic, everything that is not being affirmed in it belongs to the order of the real. On the other hand, the sense – or meaning – is the filling of the void with imaginary production. Years later, the sense is seen by Lacan as a vector, which rehabilitates sense for him in the context of his teaching. The sense as a vector differs absolutely from that which fills the void, stuffing it, to simply be a reference of direction.

---

[82] Jacques Lacan, "The Signification of the Phallus," in *Écrits*, trans. Bruce Fink (New York: Norton, 2006).

In 1976-7, Lacan observes: "There is no thing more unique than a signifier, but in a limited sense, because his value is only similar to another signifier."[83] A value of a signifier equal to the value of another signifier doesn't alter its material, its materiality. He develops it this way: "There is only a series of others, all the same as units" but in this series, the blunder will not appear in its materiality.

It is signification which alters materiality, and it is very interesting to observe that Lacan relates this to love, in the same way as he already signaled twenty years before in "The Instance of the Letter in the Unconscious or Reason Since Freud," where he says, "Love is a pebble laughing in the sun." A non-sense sentence, a metaphor that therefore gives it a whole signification, because it "recreates love in a dimension that I have said strikes me." And this is what the Cartel of the pass looks for.

And this reminds me of an experience in a Cartel of the pass: the *passant* unfolded so many signifiers which he articulated with the end of his analysis, that one could no more identify the blunder which would permit the Cartel to read a signification. It would be the non-sense of the blunder that would be able to provoke a change concerning the desire: not anymore a "desire which covers the bar making the object to emerge, but the desire to maintain, to keep that bar, and make it glow" (p.76).

This allows me to conclude that 1) what the *passeurs* passed on to us from the account of the *passant* in question, as opposed to testifying to the glow of the bar, testified to the incidence of the perennial signifiers, and 2) that when, at the core of the School, what the Cartel of the Pass is looking for is something very different.

---

[83] Jacques Lacan, *Seminar XXIII: The Sinthome*, trans. by A. R. Price (Polity, 2016)

What is at stake is not the subject in his position in the hysteric discourse – the one I placed as the *cartelisant* who launches into the transference of work with his desire to know. Nor is it the place that a +1 needs to be able to occupy from its division of being with the +1 subject in the Cartel that he is as well as the −1, the object to promote the work of the Cartel. But in the Cartel of the Pass, what we need to find is the signification, something like the empty speech, which is the bar itself to be kept in the freshness of its incandescence. The pass is not the construction of wonderful equivocal games, but the signification after the history of an analysis. It is not what is equivocal, it is just the equivocity itself. And that is what may be verified or not.

Bibliography

LACAN, J. (19..). *The Seminar, book 1, The technical writings of Sigmund Freud* (1953-54). ...

_____ (1966-67). Le Séminaire, livre XIV, La Logique du phantasme. Inedited.

_____ (1974). The Third. ....

_____ (1976-77). Le Séminaire, livre XXIV, L'Insu que sait d'une bévue que s'aille à mourre. Ineditedthe

_____ (1986). *Le Séminaire, livre VII, L'Éthique de la psychanalyse* (1959-60). Paris, Seuil.

_____ (1990). Television (1974). New York/London, Norton & Company. Translated by Denis Hollier, Rosalind Krauss, and Annette Michelson.

On the Link of Free Association and Repetition

Nate Koser

As long as the patient is in the treatment he cannot escape from this compulsion to repeat; and in the end we understand that this is his way of remembering.
Sigmund Freud "Remembering, Repeating, and Working Through"[84]

The invitation is offered in psychoanalysis that an analysand speak, and speak as freely as possible – without censorship or judgment, without consideration of topical relevance, and without concern for individual preference or comfort. This is the material upon which the analysis relies, being as it is "merely a matter of words."[85] Yet, even as Freud showed – and anyone with any familiarity with the clinic can attest – this fundamental rule of free association involves myriad challenges. Even when an analysand is able to engage in this procedure, it inevitably runs aground in either speech or through action. However, such stumbling serves as an indication of something deserving of attention, especially in a practice that concerns itself with "impediment. Failure. Split."[86]

---

[84] Sigmund Freud "Remembering, Repeating, and Working Through," in *The Standard Edition of the Complete Psychological Works of Sigmund Freud, Vol. XII*, trans. James Strachey (London: Hogarth Press, 1971), 150.

[85] Jacques Lacan, "The Direction of the Treatment and the Principles of its Power," in *Écrits*, trans. Bruce Fink (New York: Norton), 490.

[86] Jacques Lacan, *Seminar XI: The Four Fundamental Concepts of Psychoanalysis*, trans. Alan Sheridan, ed. Jacques Alain Miller (New York: Norton, 1998).

Freud pondered over this form of apparent stoppage and upon its roots in different ways. Was it due to transference? Was it merely another sign of resistance and something to be cleared away, and if so, how? Or, perhaps, was it due to something of the very nature of the unconscious that would lead this work of free association to falter and to come upon such a limit?

After numerous occasions of encountering these elements of the unconscious that seemed to "not want to be remembered,"[87] Freud eventually thought such moments to be in the order of repetition. He considered them a signal of something of the unconscious recalcitrant not only to memory, but also to interpretation – a moment when repetitive action would be substituted for remembering. With this, it began to become clear that something in the *fundamental rule* of free association worked not only in the service of remembering, historicizing, and creating links by the work of the signifier. It also worked to show the limits of such an activity, and to bring to life, as it were, yet another scene (*eine andere Schauplatz*) to which psychoanalysis had to attend.

Much has been made of the concept of repetition in psychoanalysis. Yet, from around the time of *Seminar II*[88] and through to *Seminar XI*[89], Lacan claimed that the concept of repetition was one way of conceptualizing an essential feature of the unconscious *as such*. It was of its very nature. For Lacan, the

---

[87] Sigmund Freud, "The Dynamics of Transference," in *The Standard Edition of the Complete Psychological Works of Sigmund Freud, Vol. XII*, trans. James Strachey (London: Hogarth Press, 1971), 108.

[88] Jacques Lacan, *Seminar II: The Ego in Freud's Theory and in the Technique of Psychoanalysis*, trans. Sylvana Tomselli, ed. Jacques-Alain Miller (New York: Norton, 1991).

[89] Jacques Lacan, *Seminar XI: The Four Fundamental Concepts of Psychoanalysis*, trans. Alan Sheridan, ed. Jacques-Alain Miller (New York: Norton, 1998).

concept of repetition served to ratify the indelible position of the unconscious in the symbolic – as an "insistence of speech"[90] and the signifier. This insistence, the return of the signifier in the chain, was considered proof positive of the unconscious as linguistically determined and following a logic. In *Seminar XI*, however, something is further emphasized by Lacan that both adds to and changes the concept of repetition at its base. The specificity of the concept of repetition is directed away from its quality of symbolic insistence and toward its cause.

In *Seminar XI*[91], Lacan borrowed from Aristotle the concepts *automaton* and *tuché* to address this specificity. The *automaton*, or "network of signifiers"[92] as Lacan defined it, is henceforth used to describe the symbolic insistence of the unconscious – what Lacan had previously considered essential to the concept of repetition. This symbolic insistence is precisely what is discovered through free association, through the return of those signifiers, which have come to animate the subject and make reference to desire. It is from within free association that such insistence returns. However, as Freud noted before him, Lacan reiterated that "the subject in himself, the recalling of his biography… goes only to a certain limit"[93] – even if this recalling occurs by way of parapraxes and their interpretation. As was stated earlier, the free association that introduces such signifiers brings with it its own limit.

---

[90] Jacques Lacan, *Seminar III: The Psychoses*, trans. Russell Grigg, ed. Jacques-Alain Miller (New York: Norton, 1997), 242.

[91] Jacques Lacan, *Seminar XI: The Four Fundamental Concepts of Psychoanalysis*, trans. Alan Sheridan, ed. Jacques Alain Miller (New York: Norton, 1998).

[92] *Ibid* pg. 42

[93] *Ibid* pg. 49

Rather than being solely classified as the return of the signifier through the formations of the unconscious discovered in free association, Lacan stated that fundamentally repetition is an *encounter* – "*as if by chance*"[94] – with the real that is the cause of this insistence. To be even more precise, repetition is the "missed" or "failed" encounter of *tuché*, "*the encounter with the real*"[95] to which it is always already directed. This real cause is essentially linked to the *object a*, the cause of desire and object of the drive. In so being, it is inherently sexual and pertaining to a sexual real. As Lacan put it, "the reality of the unconscious is sexual reality."[96] With this, repetition proper becomes the simultaneous missing of and search for an encounter with the *object a* "*as if by chance.*" It is not merely the symbolic insistence of signifiers, but is an encounter with the real cause that is veiled by such insistence, an encounter such insistence cannot mend or avoid.

Already in Freud, but certainly with Lacan's definition of repetition from *Seminar XI*[97] forward, it is clear that repetition has technical implications in the clinic, and such implications raise questions about free association. Through the work of free association, psychoanalysis opens the opportunity not only to address the formations of the unconscious, which present – despite their ciphered disguise – the insistence of signifiers pertaining to desire. It is also precisely through this that the analysis touches upon what is excluded from association, what lies at the limit of the signifier in its insistence: the constitutive cause of the subject of the

---

[94] *Ibid* pg. 54
[95] *Ibid* pg. 53
[96] *Ibid* pg. 150
[97] Jacques Lacan, *Seminar XI: The Four Fundamental Concepts of Psychoanalysis*, trans. Alan Sheridan, ed. Jacques Alain Miller (New York: Norton, 1998).

unconscious, the real toward which repetition tends. Due to this, the insistence of the signifier is not the whole story, because it makes reference to and circumscribes another hole, a gap, a limit to the story.

If free association is the method by which psychoanalysis introduces symbolic insistence and hits upon its real cause, how should the analysis address this cause specifically? Here, Freud and Lacan seem to differ, though there is a thread that links their perspectives. For Freud, "the main instrument...for curbing the patient's compulsion to repeat and for turning it into a motive for remembering lies in the handling of transference,"[98] and "one must allow the patient time to become conversant with this resistance with which he has now become acquainted, to *work through*[99] it, to overcome it, by continuing, in defiance of it, the analytic work according to the fundamental rule."[100] In essence, Freud understood repetition as something that could be *worked around*, as it were, by the analyst's handling of transference, and the analysand's continued efforts of free association, to get to the unconscious material implied therein regardless of its resistant nature. The handling of the transference functioned so as to permit the treating of repetition with more remembering, treating the faltering of free

---

[98] Sigmund Freud, "Remembering, Repeating, and Working Through," in *The Standard Edition of the Complete Psychological Works of Sigmund Freud, Vol. XII*, trans. James Strachey (London: Hogarth Press, 1971), 154.

[99] Here, it seems helpful to highlight Freud's term in German: *durcharbeiten*. According to Larousse, *durcharbeiten* is translated into English as "to work through," "to work without a break," and "to work one's way through," the latter as if moving oneself through a crowd. This feels an important reminder, especially for the English reader, that *working through* does not necessarily mean to dissolve, to solve, or to *get over*.

[100] Sigmund Freud, "Remembering, Repeating, and Working Through," in *The Standard Edition of the Complete Psychological Works of Sigmund Freud, Vol. XII*, trans. James Strachey (London: Hogarth Press, 1971), 155.

association with more signifiers – through either interpretation or construction, given the analysand's associative material.

For Lacan, though it is essential that the analyst handle the transference in the face of repetition and continue to direct the treatment according to the fundamental rule, it appears it is so for another kind of outcome. In *Seminar XI*[101] Lacan stated that the transference enacts the sexual reality of the unconscious, and that the transference is the vehicle through which the *object a* takes its place in the analysis.[102] Transference conjures up this lost object and this enactment is a staging of its permanence for the subject. In handling transference, the analyst allows for such an occurrence to take place. The analyst permits this staging of the subject's relation to the *object a* and, therefore, also links this staging to the free associative speech of the analysand.[103]

In repetition, however, it is the discontent inherent in the failed and missed encounter with the *object a* that arrives *"as if by chance."*[104] Handling the transference not only stages this relation to the *object a*, it also brings about this encounter of repetition of the real. In repetition, an analysand is – once again, though it is not experienced this way – shown the failure of grasping it, the limit of the real that makes such a possession impossible. To quote Lacan,

---

[101] Jacques Lacan, *Seminar XI: The Four Fundamental Concepts of Psychoanalysis*, trans. Alan Sheridan, ed. Jacques Alain Miller (New York: Norton, 1998).

[102] This is a point we see clarified even further in Lacan's construction of the *analyst's discourse* in *Seminar XVII: The Other side of Psychoanalysis*.

[103] The idea of *free* here brings to mind a lyric from Bob Dylan's, *Ballad in Plain D*. "Ah, my friends from the prison, they ask unto me/"How good, how good does it feel to be free?"/And I answer them most mysteriously/"Are birds free from the chains of the skyway?"

[104] Jacques Lacan, *Seminar XI: The Four Fundamental Concepts of Psychoanalysis*, trans. Alan Sheridan, ed. Jacques Alain Miller (New York: Norton, 1998), 54.

"the real is that which always comes back to the same place – to the place where the subject in so far as he thinks, where the *res cogitans*, does not meet it."[105] This real impossibility encountered in repetition is not something that can be undone through more free association; it cannot be treated with more signifiers since no signifier would suffice to account for its cause. If, as Lacan put it, "no praxis is more oriented towards... the kernel of the real than psychoanalysis,"[106] it is repetition that produces at least one avenue for such an encounter.

In conclusion, free association remains the fundamental rule of psychoanalysis, but not merely to introduce the insistence of signifiers indicating desire within transference. It is also the means by which something of the *"unassimilable"*[107] – something of the cause of the subject excluded from the signifier – is encountered in repetition. And, despite the apparent differences of Freud and Lacan on the matter of how to attend to such an event, what links them is the idea that to continue on in free association *in spite of* and, more importantly, *because of* this encounter with the real, is truly subversive.

Bibliography

Jacques Lacan, "The Direction of the Treatment and the Principles of its Power," in *Écrits*, trans. Bruce Fink (New York: Norton, 2006).

---

[105] Jacques Lacan, *Seminar XI: The Four Fundamental Concepts of Psychoanalysis*, trans. Alan Sheridan, ed. Jacques Alain Miller (New York: Norton, 1998), 49.
[106] *Ibid* pg. 53
[107] *Ibid* pg. 55

Jacques Lacan, *Seminar II: The Ego in Freud's Theory and in the Technique of Psychoanalysis*, trans. Sylvana Tomselli, ed. Jacques-Alain Miller (New York: Norton, 1991).

Jacques Lacan, *Seminar III: The Psychoses*, trans. Russell Grigg, ed. Jacques-Alain Miller (New York: Norton, 1997).

Jacques Lacan, *Seminar XI: The Four Fundamental Concepts of Psychoanalysis*, trans. Alan Sheridan, ed. Jacques Alain Miller (New York: Norton, 1998).

Sigmund Freud, "Remembering, Repeating, and Working Through," in *The Standard Edition of the Complete Psychological Works of Sigmund Freud, Vol. XII*, trans. James Strachey (London: Hogarth Press, 1971).

Sigmund Freud, "The Dynamics of Transference," in *The Standard Edition of the Complete PsychologicalWorks of Sigmund Freud, Vol. XII*, trans. James Strachey (London: Hogarth Press, 1971)

The Fundamental Rule and Resistance

Gabriela Zorzutti[108]

In "Observations on Transference Love,"[109] Freud, speaking of the abstinence principle, assigns the analyst this duty: to teach the patient to overcome the pleasure principle. This is introduced in the context of a development on the satisfactions, either substitutive or premature, with the pleasant diversion which intervene in the cure after a first lifting of the symptoms and which hinders its progress.

Reading this in Freud, concerning what he calls the abstinence principle, one might wonder to what extent the fundamental rule implies, on its part, the parallel aim of a similar "teaching," ie. to overcome the pleasure principle.

If the fundamental rule teaches anything, it cannot be through the content of its statements: in its theoretical or clinical formulations, the rule cannot in any way enjoin or exhort the analyzand to any transgression of the pleasure principle, except to anchor their discourse even more firmly in a pleasure economy. They would be quite happy, perhaps comforted, by the production of unpleasant statements, in a register of complacency with the demand, henceforth determined, of the rule.

---

[108] Gabriela Zorzutti is a Lacanian analyst, AMS of the IF-SPFLF, Founder of the Colorado Analytic Forum of the Lacanian Field, Director of the Clinical College of Colorado. MA in Psychoanalysis by the UNMDP, ABD in Psychoanalysis, UBA. Has been published in Argentina, Brazil, Australia and USA.

[109] Freud, S. Complete Works, Vol XII Observations on Transference Love, 1914

Now, the rule, insofar as it can be assumed to have a determining function in the structure that Lacan called "the analyst's discourse," proceeds from the ethics attached to the latter, and thus from the place of this ethic in relation to the real[110][3] ; this excludes its reduction to the office of an ideal in which the discourse concretely held by the analysand would find its guarantees of good performance.

What is the relationship, therefore, between the statements of the rule and the ethical saying that we assume it to be?

Over the years, Freud came to formulate this fundamental rule in different ways. What these different statements have in common is the extremely precise and ordered character of the series of reasons *not to* say. The instructions not to censor are never indeterminate, they point to certain invariable criteria that is valid for all subjects submitted to free association.

For instance, he dedicates a paragraph to the fundamental rule in the text "Two Encyclopaedia Articles", from 1923, where he enumerates them as follows:

".... not to hold back any idea from communication, even if: 1. it is considered too disagreeable; or 2. it is judged nonsensical; or 3. it is too unimportant, nor 4. irrelevant to what is being looked for."[111]

This is perhaps the most frequent formulation of the fundamental rule in Freud's work. Here the criteria of *saying what is disagreeable* is just one among many others. However, there are other occasions where the statement of the fundamental rule seems to have suffered an inversion of sorts, inverting the negative

---

[110] Thesis developed by Lacan on his Seminar *The Ethics of Psychoanalysis,* in the session of November 18th, 1959

[111] Freud, S. Complete Works, Vol. XVIII, Two Encyclopaedia Articles, 1923, p. 238

instruction to rule out pathological motivations. Let us look at an example of Freud's in 1913, in "On Beginning of Treatment":

You will be tempted to say to yourself this or that is irrelevant here, or is quite unimportant, or nonsensical, so that there is no need to say it. You must never give in to those criticisms, but must say them in spite of them—indeed, you must say it precisely because you feel an aversion to doing so."[112][5] He closes the paragraph adding: "Never leave anything out because, for some reason or other, it is unpleasant to say."[113]

In this case, one of the reasons to discriminate seems to be a positive guide about that which shouldn't be omitted. Instead of ignoring the pathological reasons, the analyst will take one of them as a shortcut towards a more satisfactory discourse regarding the submission to the rule.

It is likely not by chance that this tendency to particularize what shouldn't be omitted appears in a text where Freud enters an imagined dialogue with the patient, giving voice to their resistances, which he anticipates with his advice. In fact, the rule no longer appears as a reference to a law intervening from a third place regarding Freud and his patient, but it is now confused into a series of prescriptions emitted to the patient with the aim of a good use of the association that is so called "free."

Freud speaks, in the passage we have just quoted, of an unpleasantness to say for some reason. The displeasure imagined by the analysand can thus move from the excessively intimate to the quintessence of the futile, passing through cascades of purely phonetic puns, where it is clear that there is a displeasure whose

---

[112] Freud, S. Complete Works, Vol. XII On beginning of treatment, 1913 p.135
[113] Freud, S. Complete Works, Vol. XII On beginning of treatment, 1913 p.135

pleasant counterpart is, so to speak, automatic and does not escape the analysand himself.

But how can we understand the Freudian statements with regard to the fact that, in two of them, we see the outline of this movement of idealization by which the analysand seeks to realize the unpleasant at the level of the statements he produces? First of all, the question arises as to whether the unpleasantness of what Freud is talking about can be attributed to displeasure in the sense that, moreover, it is conceived by him as a signal of repressed representations encountered during the work of thought.[114]

The concept of the fundamental rule, in Freud's work, concerns in fact before anything else, the dimension of a communication in act. In two texts, at least, Freud explicitly distinguishes the process of free association from the fundamental rule[115]. Free association is introduced as a method for the production of certain ideas, the ideas that emerge in the mind, as the German term *Einfall* conveys: a technique of renunciation of reflection, of exploration of the surface, as if it were a question, says Freud, of the landscape unfolding before our eyes from the window of the compartment of a moving train; in relation to which the term of fundamental rule is introduced to designate the ways of the communication[116] of such ideas to the analyst and the command that governs it. This

---

[114] Freud, S. Complete Works, Vol. XII The Handling of Dream Interpretation, 1911

[115] Freud, S. Complete Works, Vol XVIII Two encyclopedia Articles and Petit Abrégé de la Psychoanalyse

[116] The German term *Mitteilung* can be found in most of the Freudian statements of the rule, starting with the already mentioned Two Encyclopaedia Articles, of 1923. It implies the idea of a double partition dividing the two partners of the act of communication.

distinction is essential in the process, here the chance of the analyst to fulfill this duty of teaching to overcome the pleasure principle.

We are consequently led to measure the depth of a gap dug by the Freudian formulation of the fundamental rule: between what the analysand imagines to be unpleasant and that which is unpleasant to say: a division established between a particular requirement, to say what is unpleasant, and the risk inherent in any communication of the fantasy or its offspring, to displease by saying.

The fundamental rule, therefore, delimits the field of free association by pointing to what shouldn't be omitted. It's at the beginning of treatment, when it is necessary that the rule be uttered to the patient, as Freud stresses, more than once. With the rule in place, the process can begin. The analysand will endeavor to comply with this demand.

While it seems that the analyst is simply inviting to say, this invitation is not without engaging the resistance, this is Freud's muse really. For example, again on his text, "On beginning of treatment", he states clearly that the analyst must wait long enough before communicating to the patient anything of the order of an interpretation of unconscious material. Furthermore, he insists that nothing should be said to the patient other than what is absolutely necessary for them to go on talking... *until the transference has made itself be felt as resistance.*[117]

This is a most delicate clinical point that Freud outlines, as important to the cure as the stone was for Michelangelo, for when the transference has made the turn to resistance something has happened regarding knowledge, unconscious knowledge. What

---

[117] buscar cita en on beginning of treatment

else, other than something we *know*, could be resisted in such a manner, provoke such revolts?

Freud makes note of the distance to this knowledge, the closer to it, the stronger the resistance. Therefore, resistance informs topographically, and also informs of the time to act. On this point, Freud is careful to say that the interpretation, the answer to the riddle, has to come at a precise time, just a moment before the analysand gets there on their own. Resistance informs the analyst of such a time, the time where an interpretation, laying bare (*a*)nother knowledge, can put the Truth in question…

Now, when the analyst interprets, pointing to a possible difference, via the equivocation of language, for example, this also reveals, while pointing to this other choice possible in the equation, that our analysand has chosen a way *already*. The unconscious *is* already an interpretation. Freud is relentless on this matter, this unconscious that has already chosen is the one he commands to speak through the fundamental rule. This is far from entering in conversation with the sain part of the Ego, as the post-Freudians fancied.

Freud pays very careful attention to the interplay of transference and resistance in the cure. And furthermore, it is the experience of negative transference that situates a cure on firm ground. Freud was very careful methodologically, and for him any analysis which has not traversed these torsions is under suspicion of being mere suggestion, therefore questionable at least. He is adamant that psychoanalysis has left suggestion behind as a method, due to the flagrant flaws it presented: mainly needing the physician in command for the effects to remain in place, or else they would vanish. Therefore, negative transference, or the resistant side of transference, had an immense validity for Freud, and even more, an ethical value. He believed in the knowledge of his patients, for he was closely listening to the resistance.

When reading his case histories, it is striking to see how much respect he paid to the *résons*[118] for the resistance. To follow the resistance in its development the fundamental rule is simply the most effective exercise. From the start, and by rule, nothing of the disagreeable is to be omitted.

This torsion from transference to resistance, a torsion of knowledge (*savoir*), that Freud secures with the fundamental rule, is based on the fact that a signifier is what represents a subject for another signifier; although Freud didn't put it quite like that at the time[119] it is readable in his pen.

The way Freud treats the möbius of transference-resistance is certainly on the basis of what Lacan pointed to with his later definition of the unconscious as a knowledge without a subject. Freud was interested in the position of the subject, a chosen position then, and listening to the resistance he concluded that there is a knowledge of this act, unconscious knowledge. This is the very aim of free association, to uncover these coordinates. Only that, it needs the guidance of "say that which you tend to silence," in order to bring about a kind of knowledge that is signaled by conflict, inviting resistance thus to the first dance.

---

[118] In "Function and Field of Speech and Language in Psychoanalysis" Lacan quotes Francis Ponge, who creates this beautiful amalgamation: résons, conveying both a resonance and a reason. According to Lacan this reason which resonates - thus making use of a body- is something plausible of being captured in a formulae, susceptible of formulation. This is the same reason, which many years before, he had placed in the title of his very famous writing, the Agency of the Letter or the Reason in the Unconscious since Freud.

[119] Although Freud did not put it in these terms, this is what can be read in his Dream Interpretation, or his Psychopathology of Everyday Life, or his book on the Wittz. This is why Lacan mentions that Freud advanced linguistics in Television.

The analyst has surrendered before the resistances, perhaps it would be better to say that these are irresistible to the analyst function rather, irresistible reasons, those that Freud knew how to find beyond suggestive effects. Resistances then are these reasons, reasons in the unconscious which say of a point where there is something compromised, pinched, as if in a nerve, a place from which perspective was gained… perspective in which the subject is then constrained, alienated, identified to… These pinches or fixations are painful points, sometimes in the body, sometimes in the soul, for example what hurts to have done, or to not have done.

The unfolding of free association guided by the resistance will lead to a slimming, so to speak, a shedding of identifications, of alienating interpretations, of unifying and substantiating ego tendencies, of libidinal fixations that determine circuits of *jouissance*, in short, cleansing the subject from all that subjective mud as Lacan strongly recommended.[120]

The experience of undergoing the fundamental rule is one that points increasingly to the structure of language, to its *moteriality*.[121] This mere direction of the analysand's task can be the source of resistance at times, for example when what is resisted is the eviction of the subject from the supposition of knowledge, even when the very exercise of the rule already introduces that destiny. The place of the subject in the chain of signifiers is what is supposed by the chain, what is covered, ciphered. We only know of it thanks to its failures, the places where the chain is cut, broken, interrupted.

The Freudian invention of the analytic method to explore the articulation of *savoir* that he called unconscious is, without a doubt,

---

[120] Lacan, J. My teaching.

[121] Lacan creates this neologism to point to the fact that the only substance that analysis deals with is the material of words (mot in French), hence: moterialité

most effective and very direct. For *what* responds on the side of the analyst can be delivered in different ways, and both Freud and Lacan spoke at length of the importance, in this response, of its timing, its orientation, its form. For example, if we follow Lacan's indication outlined in *L'etourdit,* interpretation should be oriented by the different levels of equivocation (of speech, of language and logical). In the case of a homophonic equivocation, for instance, which is aimed against the imaginary consistency of the significations, it is the division of the subject that comes to the fore, revealing the presence of a knowledge (*savoir)* that operates without subject, that plays without it, and determines its *jouissance.* Grammatical equivocation, on the other hand, reveals the cause of the said by pointing to it without formulating it, that is, the inherent choice in any affirmation of the analysand. Lastly, in the case of the logical equivocation, without which, as Lacan says in the aforementioned text, the interpretation would be foolish... for without something in the interpretation revealing the inconsistency or the incompleteness of the Other, things get rather dull quickly. Hence, the logical equivocation, by aiming at these impasses, brings to bear the existence of the impossible, the impossibility of a consistent, complete Other, of the fact that there is no sexual proportion. Freud had also already pointed to this matter. In *Analysis Terminable and Interminable,* in the chapter dedicated to the analysis of the analyst, he mentions that in these cases where formation is at issue, the effect of castration must be experienced many times in the cure, as many as to convince the candidate-to-analyst of the existence of the unconscious.

 The fundamental rule introduces that a subject be supposed to knowledge, and requires that the productions encountered in free association be guided by the flow of resistance. The interpretation reveals is the architexture[122] of the unconscious drawn by free association precisely where resisting, for those pinch-points, or fixations, are the places where the perspectives tense the plane, so the blueprint of the unconscious is sketched, so to speak.

The courage of the method is striking: to orient the matter towards a *savoir* that enters the field by failing, for the equivocation effect does not land in the field of reference or recognition. Furthermore, the subject is already determined and inscribed in the world as caused by a certain effect of the signifier; this renders it inept to gather what was inscribed in terms of that signifying effect, something does not add up... in these pinches, constrained and concerned perspectives are where the analyst finds a chance to put the Truth in question via the interpretation.

To put in act the subject of the unconscious is the aim of transference. The fundamental rule is uttered once transference has been established, that is, when there is a supposition to knowledge in operation, which, at the beginning of the adventure, requires a subject in order for the supposition of knowledge to function. This being the initial point of an analysis already suggests that the ego is sent for a vacation, so to speak, for this is to begin by supposing knowledge on a subject outside the ego, not the I. Here the interpretative dimension works inasmuch as the interpretation conveys a different reading of a signifying articulation in the chain that is already there. In other words, the reading that this unconscious *is* already, as Freud had said, gets a different rendering via the analyst's interpretation, so that the question of a truth other than that of intention can be posed.

---

[122] Architexture: neologism composed of archi and texture, denoting the structure and the invention of the unconscious in a space that is possible for a speaking-being to inhabit.

The standing of the analyst in this act called analytic since Lacan, that of bearing transference, in the establishment of an operative supposition of a subject to knowledge – knowing thanks to their own experience of having finished their own itinerary, and being aware of the elusive fate that they are led to – depends on how firmly they oblige themselves to the discipline of "restricting every support of the subject to its grammatical existence."[123]

If knowledge (*savoir*) seems to need the supposition of a subject at the beginning, this is only to find that this knowledge works without it, even fails it! The task of associating freely, which the analyst causes in their analysand by way of the fundamental rule, is a task that already implies in itself the destitution of this subject initially supposed to knowledge which awaits in the final horizon of the analytic adventure, to recommence, to be reinvented each time.

To illustrate this with Lacan's own words, from his seminar on the Analytic Act, in the session of 1/24/68, while commenting on the difference between a doing that is purely of words and an act as the limit of interpretation, he says:

(...) in the technique, in that which seems to be nothing, that famous free association could easily be translated as the signifier in act, if we look at things closely, that is, that the true sense of the fundamental rule is: that the subject be absent. Here we see the task, letting the signifier do its thing – this is the doing of the subject.[124]

Since Lacan we are aware of a consequence of language of major ethical relevance, which responds to the question on the relationship between the statements of the rule and the ethical saying that we assume it to be. In the words of Gabriel Lombardi:

---

[123] Lacan, J. The Analytic Act, p. 105, unpublished
[124] Lacan, J. The Analytic Act, p. 112, unpublished

"(...)language not only structures the *parlêtre*, at the same time that it structures him, it renders him potentially free of any coercion of language... and other subjections. (...) This being carries within itself, as effect of the structure of language, and thanks to it, the anguishing possibility of parting with any coercion, biological, social, moral or merely of language – those demands that drive in him with the insistence that we all experience in our own flesh."[125]

But then, how does the analyst teach their patient to overcome the pleasure principle? By inviting this subject of the unconscious, of grammatical support, to speak. By way of the enforcement of the fundamental rule – which will set in act not the I, but the "I am not if I speak" – the subject of the unconscious is put in act in a psychoanalysis. This is a one way trip...

Bibliography

Sigmund Freud, "The Handling of Dream Interpretation," *The Standard Edition of the Complete Psychological Works of Sigmund Freud, Vol.* XII, trans. James Strachey (London: Hogarth Press, 1957

Sigmund Freud, "Observations on Transference Love," *The Standard Edition of the Complete Psychological Works of Sigmund Freud, Vol.* XII, trans. James Strachey (London: Hogarth Press, 1957)

Sigmund Freud, "On beginning of Treatment," *The Standard Edition of the Complete Psychological Works of Sigmund Freud, Vol.* XII, trans. James Strachey (London: Hogarth Press, 1957

---

[125] Lombardi, G. El metodo Clinico en la perspectiva analitica. Paidos, 2018, p. 33-34

Sigmund Freud, "Two Encyclopaedia Articles," *The Standard Edition of the Complete Psychological Works of Sigmund Freud, Vol.* XVIII, trans. James Strachey (London: Hogarth Press, 1957)

Sigmund Freud, "Papers on Technique," *The Standard Edition of the Complete Psychological Works of Sigmund Freud, Vol.* XII, trans. James Strachey (London: Hogarth Press, 1957)

Jacques Lacan, "The Ethics of Psychoanalysis" The Seminar, Book VII, trans. Dennis Porter (NYC, Norton & Company, 1997)

Jacques Lacan, "Function and Field of Speech and Language in Psychoanalysis" *Ecrits, A selection*, trans. Alan Sheridan (New York, Norton & Company Inc, 1977)

Jacques Lacan, "The Agency of the Letter or the Reason in the Unconscious since Freud" *Ecrits, A selection*, trans. Alan Sheridan (New York, Norton & Company Inc, 1977)

Jacques Lacan, "My teaching", trans. David Macey, (NYC, Verso, 2008)

Jacques Lacan, "Television, a Challenge to the Psychoanalytic Establishment", trans. Hollier, Krauss, Michelson (NYC, Norton Press, 1990)

Colette Soler, *Lacanian Affects,* trans. Bruce Fink, (NYC, Routledge, 2016)

The Impossibilities to Free Association

Barbara Shuman

For Freud, free association was defined as speaking as freely as possible, without judgment or censorship. The patient is required to put himself in the position of a "dispassionate self-observer," not holding back any thoughts. He is encouraged to make a duty of the most complete honesty, determined not to withhold any idea from communication, even if (1) he feels that it is too disagreeable or if (2) he judges that it is nonsensical or (3) too unimportant or (4) irrelevant to what is being looked for. It is uniformly found that precisely those ideas which provoke these last-mentioned reactions are of particular value in discovering the forgotten material.

Freud discovered that by working through memories, the "dispassionate self-observer" may thus have access to forgotten material, offering the patient the aim of remembering, and not repeating, what 'lies' at the source of his suffering. This method was suggested to patients after Freud realized that hypnosis had limitations in uncovering unconscious materials. (Freud, 1923)

But how much freedom does the patient have in doing so, if he has a passion for repeating what makes him suffer? Free association continues to be the fundamental rule of any analytic treatment, and yet it appears that there is a time in each treatment where the ability to speak as freely as possible encounters resistance and impossibilities.

In this paper, I wish to explore these impossibilities. At what moment does free association fluctuate between a rambling of nonsensical verbiage and an impossibility for the subject to submit himself to the fundamental rule? Through free association, the unconscious is making itself known to the patient, whether he may hear it or not.

Language as a Structure

In the clinic, the analyst is witness to the emergence of the unconscious through speech, through signifiers as well as unconscious mechanisms where the subject shows his division, his symptom. Colette Soler, in her book, the *Unconscious Reinvented*, says that the unconscious is Freudian, as its way of access is related to the practice of speech that Freud developed: specifically, free association (Soler, 2014)[126]. What Lacan called "formations of the unconscious," including slips of the tongue, parapraxes, bungled acts, etc, have a 'je ne sais quoi,' a quality that cannot be described or named easily. It is a sense of the uncanny that takes the subject by surprise. The subject arrives at a juncture where the familiar and the strangeness in speech collide.

While Lacan says, "the unconscious is structured as a language,"[127] this does not mean it can be articulated by the subject, or that there are not aspects of language that remain merciless to the subject who encounters, when the he least expects it, the imposed structure of language. The subject may feel powerless, speechless, as if he becomes seized with a libidinal impediment, where what may be expressed becomes inarticulable.

---

[126] Find source
[127] J. Lacan (1966) Ecrits. Editions du Seuil. Paris, FR.

Conditions for Free Association:

Psychoanalysis is commonly known as 'talk therapy.' Based on this simple description, it is assumed that as long as the patient speaks, a cure can begin and have desirable effects of appeasing the complaint or suffering that the patient brings to analysis.

If only this were so simple! When Freud discovered this method through working with hysterics, it was after other methods of treatment that relied primarily on suggestion— especially hypnosis—were ineffective in leading to a cure. The patient, while speaking "freely," could unravel repressed materials of the unconscious and find the source of his symptom. Through slips of the tongue and other parapraxes, unconscious material was revealed in a manner provided by no other clinical technique.

If psychoanalysis were only 'talk therapy,' based on the assumption that this technique relies exclusively on the words that the patient says, we would remain in the realm of a therapeutic intervention, where just the act of speaking would bring a cathartic effect of immediate relief.

Freud warns us about this fundamental mistake in his paper, "The Beginning of Treatment,"[128] as he soon found that free association came with interferences, limitations, and barriers that were carried out by the *patient himself.* Something beyond words— a silence, a hesitation, a stumbling, a lapse, or an instance of utterance that would bring the advancement of the treatment to a halt—intercedes to make speech suddenly impossible. The patient's capacity to continue applying the fundamental rule grinds to a fixated state. Even as hysterics would see their physical symptoms

---

[128] S. Freud (1913). "On the Beginning the Treatment," Standard Edition of the Complete Psychological Works of Sigmund Freud. Volume XII. The Hogarth Press. London, UK.

disappear, the root of the symptom formation remained buried under a layer of psychic mechanisms meant to keep unspeakable and intolerable material at bay. In other words, repression.

The Limits of Free Association

In terms of mental health treatment, the experience that one encounters when beginning a psychoanalysis is like no other. There are no specific guidelines, treatment plans or goals set by the analyst. The only condition that the patient is asked to follow is the one of speaking as freely as possible.

Free associate. If we look a bit closer to those two words, one can see that their pairing is odd. Derived from Latin, the word *associates* means to unite, to ally. Chemistry and other sciences speak of association as a connection, a bond between two particles, entities that, when united, form a unit or a link.

Freedom can be seen, in the capitalist world, as to act and think without constraint, independently from others or authorities. Thus, in psychoanalysis, to free associate is the ability to speak without restraint, to associate a chain of words that, when linked to others, can reveal unconscious material. As "freely as possible" means without judgment or censorship, either the patient's own or that which he is subject to in the course of living in civilization. How are these two terms, "free" and "association," linked in psychoanalysis and what kind of impossibilities does this fundamental rule encounter?

Freedom in Psychoanalysis

I will speak of the apparent freedom or lack of it mostly from the side of the patient upon beginning an analysis. Even if the analyst's only request is for the patient to apply the fundamental rule, the analysand-neurotic soon finds out that his free will is at stake, and that, though he thought he could speak freely, he finds himself instead encapsulated by the limitations of language itself. Here, language as the structure of the Real unconscious, forces the subject to make a choice: speak or to remain silent.

Gabriel Lombardi, an Argentinean analyst and writer of numerous books on psychoanalysis, wrote about this dilemma of freedom in the psychoanalytic treatment. If we apply Lombardi's ideas on freedom to the technique of free association, we can see that free association has a cost that, at the beginning, appears to deplete the neurotic of his resources.[129] Lombardi explains that the concepts of psychoanalysis, its ethics and practice, allows to the patient a "privileged access" to choose. Free association offers a method where the subject succumbs as a "parlêtre," accepts the wager regardless of whether he can freely choose what he has to say. By doing so, he will realize that his associative freedom has limits. Impossibilities arise as he begins to hear himself speak.

Words, Signification, Signifiers

Free association is not just words. Everyone can speak, although when someone is in analysis, this act at times, as I've shown, becomes difficult it itself. At that moment, the subject can realize that what was once a natural effect of learning a language—precisely how to speak—becomes a stumbling in which the one who speaks does not have the same freedom. He listens to his own speech for the equivocations it imposes. Words become consequential, and have substantial effects. Signifiers trace a mark that the patient

---

[129] G. Lombardi (2008). Predeterminación y Libertad Electiva. Revista Universitaria de Psicoanálisis. Buenos Aires, AR

continues to stumble upon against his will, as if he had never heard himself speak before.

In analysis, the patient becomes not only a being who speaks, but experiences himself as "a speaking being," finding where his suffering has become the detritus of signification, as he is host to a litany of signifiers that serve to represent him as a subject for other signifiers, and for these, alone. Gabriel Lombardi speaks about this lack of freedom, which makes the term "free association" a contradiction that can mark the first limitation of language. Lombardi explains:

The patient repeats the associations, returns to the same thing, repeats instead of remembering, blindly acts out a failed encounter. This last form of repetition is called transference by Freud, and refers to the moment when the subject loses his associative freedom - nothing really occurs to him - in order to link himself to the presence of the listener. This has a methodological advantage, since it allows the analyst, by interpreting, to reinforce the fundamental rule, to propitiate the opening of new associative strata that were hitherto disconnected or repressed. So, with his interpretation, capable of opening surprising associative doors, the analyst treats the analysand as a being capable of choosing even beyond what he knows, betting that the limits that the subject finds in the exercise of his associative freedom should not necessarily be forever those currently imposed on him by the compulsion to repetition.[130]

The subject in analysis has thus a choice, not only to speak, but also to face the horror of his speech that reveals the disproportion

---

[130] G. Lombardi (2007). La Clínica del Psicoanálisis. Vol 1. Etica y Técnica. Edición Atuel. Buenos Aires, AR

and often inaccuracy of his actions and words, or to remain blind in front of his own resistance.

When Freud discovered the method of free association, he realized that its aim wasn't only to make someone speak about the immediate complaint of his suffering. The subject was also accompanied by a body, one that also spoke with jouissance. For Lacan, jouissance was what interfered with the ability to free associate, thus revealing signifiers that would continue to repeat themselves despite the wanting or willing of the patient. In *Television*, Lacan says that "the unconscious speaks, which makes it dependent on language." [131] Thus, contrary to undomesticated animals, the speaking being is encapsulated in a body that speaks of a symptom that could not exist without jouissance, and that jouissance could not occur without the body that is bathed in language.

Lombardi restates this idea when he says that: "The body is the only place where the symptom can be elaborated in analysis, which is the hysterical symptom."[132] (2007) This hysterization of symptoms is also true of obsessional neurotics, as Freud discovered through the process of free association with both hysterical and obsessional cases.

Within the structure of language—its enunciations, significations, the inevitable slides along chains of signifiers—the subject appears trapped, an agent acting against his own will and with an (apparent) lack of either satisfaction or desire.

Among the impossibilities for the patient to apply the fundamental rule lies also this: the subject is faced not only with a certain psychical reality, but also with the structure of language itself

---

[131] J. Lacan (1974) Television. Editions du Seuil. Paris, FR
[132] Ibid

in the guise of the unconscious, an initially—before an analysis—unspeakable knowledge without a subject. The "realities" of certain choices that were impossible to make, i.e., choosing one's parents, choosing to be born, choosing the culture in which one was raised—all of these and more comprise the particular labyrinth the subject faces as he begins to decipher the knowledge and contingencies of the unconscious.

The subject also cannot choose the signification of more complex struggles, such as with or against time, death, with or against urges such as hunger and thirst, travails of being encapsulated in a body that has also—and is nothing beyond— its own limitations. From this, Lacan speaks of the encounter with the Real, meaning the state of nature that is forever severed by the entrance into language. For Freud, instincts were an organism's return to an earlier state, but it is only through language that instinct becomes the constant pulse of the drive. The constancy of drives in face of the failure of their satisfaction, and the subsequent displacement of libidinal objects, marks a complexity of human existence that has no analogy in nature.

In that sense, free association has a semblance of illusion for the subject who thinks that he only speaks to say whatever he wants, whatever he wills, until words escape him, until they are missing when it comes to those residues and the suffering that cannot (yet) be transformed into speech.

Resistance, Repetition, Symptom

In psychoanalysis, the one who chooses what to talk about is the patient. The analyst does not provide prompts or other restrictions that would lead the patient to speak or give emphasis upon one particular topic. On the contrary, without any guidance but to speak freely, the patient encounters his very own limitations, ones that free association in fact provoke. Through this (re)encounter with castration, the patient comes face to face precisely with his resistance, bringing to light a conflict proper for the one who speaks.

In obsessional neurosis, for example, the conflict points to the difficulty for the subject who must choose—yet, he doesn't. The patient repeats associations, goes in circles, loses himself in a blah-blah that points to what repeats instead of being remembered. In that sense, free association is called the fundamental rule in as much as it is fundamental for the symptom to appear and be articulated. In obsessional neurosis, free association illuminates what it is in the subject that resists, repeats, and creates countless obstacles. Free association is, then, a semblance of freedom, where the will of the patient becomes compromised when he realizes it is not he who is the one who governs language, but that it is language that governs him.

That the imperatives of language are found in what the subject repeats is seen in the clinic over and over again, as the treatment winds its way through equivocation, lapses, or forgetfulness. In hysteria, for example, what returns from the repressed is lodged in the body with the formation of a symptom that goes beyond the tale of a fantasy. Freud made the discovery that beyond the streaming words of free association, there is a body that speaks, and an unconscious that does not lie.

Looking more closely at the fundamental rule of psychoanalysis, free association, it becomes apparent that a psychoanalysis, at least a real one, could not exist without it.

But the analyst's listening encompasses a multitude of other tasks.

When the analyst asks the future analysand to speak whatever comes to his mind, it is not only to listen to his literal words. It is also a listening to the position of the subject in relation to his world. It is a listening to the body, to the peculiar opening and closing of the unconscious, to the enunciation, and to the demand.

Conclusion

Free association can be seen as an analytic *dispositif* that combines the inner and outer dimensions that go into make us speaking-beings. It is very far from the idea that humans have instincts. The analyst hears the pulsation of the drive beyond the words of his analysand. He hears the position of the subject in regards to his symptoms, his association to others, and with the Other. He marks well the analysand's compulsive repetition to continue to suffer. Through the desire of the analyst, words become a body of jouissance, and a place where a subject is divided. It is where the psyche becomes compromised as the unconscious reveals itself to the patient. Free association becomes then the link between the patient and the cure, the compass that guides the analyst not only to intervene but to act according to an ethical position that he, himself, discovered through applying the fundamental rule in his own analysis.

Bibliography

S. Freud (1913). On the Beginning the Treatment. Standard Edition of the Complete Psychological Works of Sigmund Freud. Volume XII. The Hogarth Press. London, UK.

S. Freud (1923). Two Encyclopaedia Articles. Standard Edition of the Complete Psychological Works of Sigmund Freud. Volume XVIII. The Hogarth Press. London, UK.

J. Lacan (1966) Ecrits. Editions du Seuil. Paris, FR.

J. Lacan (1974) Television. Editions du Seuil. Paris, FR

G. Lombardi (2008). Predeterminación y Libertad Electiva. Revista Universitaria de Psicoanálisis. Buenos Aires, AR

G. Lombardi (2007). La Clínica del Psicoanálisis. Vol 1. Etica y Técnica. Edición Atuel. Buenos Aires, AR

C. Soler (2014). The Unconscious Reivented. Routledge. New-York, NY

Free Association and Mourning

Michael McAndrew

Within the United States, there are as many therapies available for the consumer as there are flavors of soda. Two such popular "flavors" of psychotherapy are euphemistically called grief counseling and trauma therapy. In these particular therapies, the patient is encouraged by their therapist (often some sort of specialist touting advanced training or a certificate) not to freely associate, but to keep their words mainly to the grief or trauma that brought them into this professional's office in the first place.

This grief or trauma often involves a loss, usually of a loved one. Perhaps a violent situation occurred and the patient is "a survivor," and so requires specialized treatment in order to help set them back to rights. In any case, no matter the treatment, it is usually not one of psychoanalysis, as these therapies are meant to stick to the "topic" and are often limited in scope and in the number of sessions. Though the therapy itself may be brief, Freud writes in *Mourning and Melancholia* (1916-1917 [1915]) that mourning itself is not.

Freud writes, "[i]n mourning we found that the inhibition and loss of interest are fully accounted for by the work of mourning in which the ego is absorbed...[i]n mourning it is the world which has become poor and empty..." (Freud, 1916). After the death of a loved one, or a profound trauma, there is a drawing in of libido, as Freud tells us, and it may be hard for the patient to talk about much else besides this event. However, this should be no excuse for the patient to stay within that territory. The patient can be invited to say more through the free association of a psychoanalysis. It may even be that this trauma and grief counseling could exacerbate the role that loss takes in the patient's psyche; already outsized, the trauma therapist encourages the patient to stare into the sun that is their loss.

In three papers published successively, "Thoughts for the Times on War and Death" (1915), "On Transience" (1916), and the aforementioned "Mourning and Melancholia" (1916-17), Freud outlines a paradigm far different than those pursued by the programmatics available to a subject in mourning today. This approach offers a chance, with no guarantee, of being able to freely work through their mourning, in their own time. This inaugurates a possibility of the mourner to live their life with desire, sans the beloved object, in a different way. What alternative can psychoanalysis offer besides a prescription to speak about anything *but* mourning?

The standard of grief counseling is often prescribed for those subjects who have recently had a loss in their life, be it a parent, a child, even a pet. Also called bereavement counseling, it is designed to help the subject in question cope or deal with a loss. Grief, loss, bereavement, and mourning are all normalized, rather than made particular to the subject. Grief counseling is predicated on the assumption that one works through grief in stages.

In "Thoughts for the Times on War and Death" (Freud, 1915), Freud writes that the inevitability of everyone's death is reduced by an emphasis on those deaths that are sudden; be it an accident or some other misfortune, as though death can be avoided.

The complement to this cultural and conventional attitude towards death is provided by our complete collapse when death has struck down someone who we love – a parent, or partner in marriage, a brother or sister, a child or a close friend. Our hopes, our desires, and our pleasures lie in the grave with him, we will not be consoled, we will not fill the lost one's place. We behave as if we were a kind of Asra, who dies when those they love die (Freud 1915).

Freud called this mourning of a loved one "a great riddle," and said that the loss of one's love object is a mysterious and painful process (Freud, 1916) and, in light of this, not so easily treated.

What I would like to draw attention to is a much less remarked upon paper, Freud's 1916 work, "On Transience."

"On Transience" was written in the midst of a time of vast mourning during the First World War. At the time, two of Freud's sons were serving in the war, on the side of Central Powers, in the service of the Austro-Hungarian empire. Freud writes of a conversation with a friend of his, an unnamed poet. Freud sets the scene as follows:

Some time ago, in the company of a silent friend and a young, already well-known poet, I took a walk through a flourishing summer landscape. The poet admired the beauty of nature around us, but without enjoying it. He was bothered by the thought that all this beauty was destined to die away, that it would have vanished in the winter, but so would every human beauty and all the beauty and nobility that men have created and could create. Everything he would otherwise have loved and admired seemed to him devalued by the transience for which it was fated (Freud, 1916).

From the knowledge that death is the end of all things, two impulses can emanate. The first is the impulse of the young poet; a weariness with the world, a resignation, a living death, if you will. In many ways, this has become more common since the World Wars; a major disillusionment of those who have fallen away from the social bond has become generalized today. In *Lacanian Affect: the Function of Affect in Lacan's Work* (2016), Colette Soler refers to this anguish, such as experienced by the young poet, as "the shame of being alive" (Soler, p. 96, 2016). It is the kind of mourning known by "those who managed to escape from concentration camps, survivors of...World War II" (Soler, p. 96, 2016).

The other impulse is to deny that one's loved objects (and oneself) are transient, and finite. "No," Freud writes, "it is impossible that all these glories of nature and of art, ...should really melt into nothing." This resignation, that somehow these things would be spared, is a denial of death, an equally untenable position.

Both of these mental impulses place the value of these objects over time. In one case objects are worthless because they are transient. In the second case, they can somehow be preserved from death. Both are a denial of the reality of transience that Freud asserts. "The value of transience is a rarity in time. The restriction in the possibility of enjoyment increases its preciousness" (Freud, 1916).

In a clinic of the loss of children, this transience comes to bear quite suddenly. The death of an infant, a still birth, a miscarriage- though the span of the life of these may be measured from months to moments, each moment is remembered painfully, and with clarity. These moments burn all the more brightly in the minds of the mother who still treasures this lost child, no matter how brief her time as a mother to that child. As Freud states: "A flower that blossoms only for a single night does not seem to us on that account less lovely." (Freud, 1916). This does not mean the loss is any less profound, or painful, but that, perhaps through a psychoanalytic treatment, the loss can (with no guarantee) come to be valued differently in time.

The demands often placed on an analyst in this setting are of empathy and understanding. 'Have you experienced a loss like this?

Do you have children?,' implicitly, will you understand me as a woman, as a mother, as someone who experienced loss. Let's note here it is not the understanding of the other – indeed, empathy – that will gain ground here in the treatment. The loss of a child affects the body and the psyche of the mother so profoundly that it is un-understandable: words fail, especially when addressed to the other. A fairly common complaint heard in this clinic is about the "sticky" empathy of someone else trying to understand and empathize with the mother's loss, or even worse, to compare their own experience. Though two women could have lost children in situations that might seem the same according to age or manner of death of the child, they are categorically not, and these subjects will be all too quick to tell you so. The axiom that each case is one by one is recognized in this clinic with urgency, as an imperative of the treatment. It is here we can discuss this imperative, the only imperative of psychoanalysis that of free association. To move away from the stickiness of predetermined social and cultural narratives that programmatics encourage, and to the free associations of the subject; of speaking about the loss in their own way, rather than that of the other.

There are many ways children can die, from the first weeks of pregnancy into their infancy and childhood. Roughly one in four pregnancies may end in a miscarriage in the first eight to twelve weeks. Further, of women who miscarry, there is an increased risk of miscarriages in future pregnancies of up to twenty percent, according to the Mayo Clinic. This is not even to account for various genetic abnormalities or serious health conditions that may require termination of a pregnancy, either because of the risk to the mother's health upon delivery, or the quality of life of the child with such abnormalities. Factor this further with issues during delivery that may result in the death of a child during labor, as well as the period after the birth.

The demand then, on the analyst, as the subject supposed to know in a clinic such as this, is sometimes an urgent one. Many demands for sense come in the form of questions bombarding the analyst: why did my baby die? Am I a bad mother? Was I (or my body) responsible for their death in some way? Will I ever be able to have children again? This one is a particularly poignant question in the case of multiple miscarriages or those experiencing the failure in vitro fertilization or other artificially assisted reproductive methods.

Freud, in his "Recommendations to Physicians Practicing Psycho-Analysis" (1912) advises his colleagues to "model themselves on the surgeon" who "puts aside all feelings, even his human sympathy, and concentrates his mental forces on the single aim of performing the operation as skillfully as possible" (Freud, 1912). In this clinic especially, Freud's recommendation is crucial. He continues: "A surgeon of earlier times took as his motto the words: *Je le pansai, Dieu le gerit* ("I dressed his wounds, God cured him"). The analyst should be content with something similar" (Freud, 1912).

The analyst invites the patient to assiduously follow the fundamental rule of the treatment: to say everything that comes to mind, no matter how strange it might seem, without censorship. It is the responsibility of the analyst to receive this information with evenly suspended attention, without directing the treatment to the grief (in these cases, the loss of a child), but rather anywhere the patient's associations may follow. Lacan writes in the "Direction of the Treatment and the Principles of Its Power," the analyst must direct the treatment, not the patient. As relates to a treatment of mourning, particularly of the loss of one's child, and free associations' role in it, I will return once more to Freud's remarks "On Transience," which are applicable in these cases of mourning and grief.

Mourning, as we know, however painful it may be, comes to a spontaneous end…when once the mourning is over…we shall build up again all that has…[been] destroyed, and perhaps on firmer ground and more lasting than before.

Bibliography

Sigmund Freud, "Mourning and Melancholia," *The Standard Edition of the Complete Psychological Works of Sigmund Freud, Vol.* XIV, trans. James Strachey (London: Hogarth Press, 1957)

Sigmund Freud, "On Transience," *The Standard Edition of the Complete Psychological Works of Sigmund Freud, Vol.* XIV, trans. James Strachey (London: Hogarth Press, 1957)

Sigmund Freud, "Thoughts for the Times on War and Death," *The Standard Edition of the Complete Psychological Works of Sigmund Freud, Vol.* XIV, trans. James Strachey (London: Hogarth Press, 1957)

Sigmund Freud, "Papers on Technique," *The Standard Edition of the Complete Psychological Works of Sigmund Freud, Vol.* XII, trans. James Strachey (London: Hogarth Press, 1957)

Colette Solar, *Lacanian Affects,* translated by Bruce Fink, (Routledge, 2016)

Freud's "Bias": Notes on Psychical Determinism

Michael Barnard

In *Five Lectures in Psychoanalysis*,[133] delivered extempore at Clark University and then reluctantly recomposed by Freud into this slight and essential volume, he begins the third lecture in a strange way: " – It is not always easy to tell the truth," he says, "especially when one has to be concise; and I am thus today obliged to correct a wrong statement that I made in my last lecture."

He continues:

I said to you that, having dispensed with hypnosis, I insisted on my patients nevertheless telling me what occurred to them in connection with the subject under discussion, and assured them that they really knew everything that they had ostensibly forgotten and that the idea that occurred to them would infallibly contain what we were in search of; and I went on to say to you that I found that the first idea occurring to my patients did in fact produce the right thing and turned out to be the forgotten continuation of the memory. This, however, is not in general the case, and I only put the matter so simply for the sake of brevity. Actually it was only for the first few times that the right thing which had been forgotten turned up as a result of simple insistence on my part. When the

---

[133]Sigmund Freud, Five Lectures on Psycho-Analysis in The Standard Edition of the Complete Psychological Works of Sigmund Freud, Vol. XI, trans. James Strachey (London:Hogarth Press, 1971).

procedure was carried further, ideas kept on emerging that could not be the right ones...and I found myself once more regretting my abandonment of hypnosis.[134]

Why does he say this to his audience? Not only does the contradiction bring questions concerning the speaker's reliability, but it also casts into doubt the efficacy of the entire enterprise of free association. Can we attribute Freud's approach in the "Third Lecture" to a rhetorical flourish of Continental decorum on display for his illustrious American audience? Or does he give voice here to an anguish, a conflict that is deeply seated in the mind of the founder of psychoanalysis? Perhaps we might even call it a symptom. For careful reading gives rise to the suspicion that there is something "telling" about Freud's account of the struggle to establish free association as the clinical approach to analyzing the repressed representations of the unconscious.

What Freud is describing in 1909 is the coming of age of psychoanalysis, the crucial point in its history, where he outlines the discovery of free association, the practice of asking and insisting that the patient speak the first thought in his minds, without dismissing or censoring its content. And he admits he was at quite a loss.

"I clung to a prejudice," he says.

I am bound to say that it is sometimes useful to have prejudices. I cherished a high opinion of the strictness with which mental processes are determined, and I found it impossible to believe that an idea produced by a patient...could be an arbitrary one...[135]

While he has earlier, in the second lecture, introduced the theory of repression based on the observable effects of resistance,

---

[134] Ibid, p. 29.
[135] Ibid, p. 29.

Freud implies he mistakenly expected the work of free association to provide a reliable access to repressed memories or fantasies of the patient, which he believed must be forcing through from the unconscious, resulting in the symptom. He admits that, while what he calls here the "main rule of psycho-analysis" can and does bear immediate fruit in this direction, the effect in the treatment is limited and short-lived. As promising as he initially found the introduction of free association into the clinic, he discovered his pursuit of the elusive wish or memory rejected by consciousness was inevitably derailed.

However, Freud noted that the pursuit failed in a manner unlike the ultimately disappointing results achieved through treating hysteria with hypnosis and suggestion. In the cases where treatment was by means of free association (beginning in the mid-1890s, when there wasn't yet a name for the approach),[136][4] inevitably there appeared in his writing about these treatments what he termed "resistance," a force that denied the patient conscious access to his own thoughts and memories.

It is Freud's own self-proclaimed prejudice (or symptom, or act of faith, as we might say it, which all sounds strange when applied to the works of Freud), and which I am referring to as a bias, that interests me. It catches my attention as a reader of Freud, but also as an analyst. Why does he sound so nervous? And what is the point of his "confession"?

I sense it is because there is a logical gap for which he cannot yet account. He arrived upon this gap when he was compelled to inaugurate free association, to bring his patients to speak the first thoughts to come into their minds, despite the negligible effects he

---

[136] Ernest Jones, *The Life and Works of Sigmund Freud* (Penguin 1964) p. 214

was empirically encountering in the clinic. Understandably, this provoked great frustration for Freud as a scientist. And yet, the result of persisting beyond his own credulity was that he began to listen more freely and move further from his own earlier assumptions.

Freud begins listening at this point, essentially, to signifiers, as they are manifest by the symptom, instead of following the patient's narrational threads of signification. He does so by coming to recognize the topological value provided as the symptom, which, if allowed, would precisely locate its own limits, and reveal the schemes of its resistances.

Freud writes:

The idea which occurred to the patient in place of what we were in search of had thus itself originated like a symptom: it was a new, artificial and ephemeral substitute for what had been repressed, and was dissimilar to it in proportion to the degree of distortion it had undergone under the influence of the resistance...The idea occurring to the patient must be in the nature of an *allusion* to the repressed element, like a representative of it in indirect speech."[137]

Contrary to the ideals of psychotherapy or contemporaneous theories of incapacity on the part of the psychical apparatus, Freud's theory of repression was explained "dynamically, from the conflict of opposing mental forces...the outcome of an active struggling on the part of the two psychical groupings against each other."[138] Thus, the greater the resistance to the repressed idea, the more intractably bound the idea was to the unconscious wish constantly pressing to

---

[137] Sigmund Freud, Five Lectures on Psycho-Analysis in The Standard Edition of the Complete Psychological Works of Sigmund Freud, Vol. XI, trans. James Strachey (London: Hogarth Press, 1971), p. 30.
[138] Ibid, p. 26.

break through repression. This is a quantitative calculation of a libidinal economy that relates to the laws of thermodynamics, perhaps the most deterministic laws in all of science. The calculations Freud is describing were instrumental in his theories of the Pleasure Principle and the primary and secondary processes.

However, discovering precisely what is most peculiar to a patient's symptom – how and where repression fails, the gaps in the scaffolding of fantasy that sustains the subject – also opens a new territory for psychoanalytic investigation. Through the praxis of free association, an assemblage of topological content emerges, the patient's own and particular *terroir* of defenses.

Because, through free association, "nothing can occur [to the patient] which is not in an indirect fashion dependent on the complex we are in search of,"[139] he calls this method the "only practicable one."[140]

The product of free association was not a catalog of narratives to be collected, investigated and used to explain the ego to itself. The process was both more arduous and impossible. The product was found exclusively, in fact, in mining the materials deemed most useless and deplorable by the patient himself. Indeed, more than once Freud compared the work with excavation, archeological and otherwise:

This associative material, which the patient contemptuously rejects when he is under the influence of the resistance instead of under the doctor's, serves the psycho-analyst, as it were, as ore from

---

[139] Ibid, p. 32.
[140] Ibid, p. 32.

which, with the help of some simple interpretative devices, he extracts its content of precious metal.[141]

The kernel of the discovery is, then, not a means to access the contents of the unconscious directly, as through techniques of hypnosis. Nor is it an attempt to access these contents indirectly, through invoking them surreptitiously, as it were, teasing out content through a cathartic and chaotic purge of memories and associations (as in, "say it all and eventually the right representations will pop out"). Instead, free association serves to make the patient stumble into acts of parapraxis. And this is because these acts, these "mistakes" – especially as they appear clinically in numerous guises, from slips in speech to renditions of dreams, accidents, jokes – are inevitably determined to speak particularly in each *parlétre* or subject. The subject, whose being it is to be "spoken," i.e., exists once, and only when, and in the determined manner of, a particular body that speaks. Not only can it not be another, it's ex-istence is purely dynamic, contingent on conflicting meanings of sense. Psychoanalysis, singularly, can reveal the "sense" of irreconcilable meanings, if only through the "knowing" or limit of that which is persistently being, and has forever been – lost.

ii

Had he been a late-modern era researcher, the deterministic element of Freud's discovery would have been by his own admission contaminated by what's called, "researcher's bias." But the focus of Freud's inquiry was exclusive to his own clinic, measured in terms of fidelity to the work of the symptom and of the alleviation of psychical suffering. His method emerged out of decades of treating

---

[141] Ibid, p. 32.

patients, and documenting cases, and this as a prescribed cure was met at least initially with mixed and perplexing results. But with the introduction of free association and consequential changes in Freud's conception of the unconscious, psychoanalysis was established.

Perhaps ironically this was accomplished, in the end, by the basis of an unshakable prejudice that Freud had in psychical determinism, and the more radical notion that preexisting structures of symptoms embedded in the layers, as it were, of the psychical dispositif can be treated via speech. This bias – arguably a symptom in and of itself, in that it was in essence a compromise for Freud with methods of science – was what, through the birth of free association, shifted the landscape in the treatment of symptomatic mental illness. It was an earthquake that determines even today the terrain where the therapists build their ticky-tacky houses, each one just like another, molds for evidence-based psychotherapy.

No saying can be arbitrary, and even as the subject says a conscious untruth he enunciates truly the position of his desire. Even, and especially, in the negations the subject articulates.[142]

That no saying can be arbitrary means there is a particular metonymy of "senses," that marks a trail to wherever the subject has passed, and returns again and again. It means that potentially everything of the subject's psychic reality is connected and all of it can be discovered and everything (if only one has the "code") can be "read."

(Let us pause briefly to wonder – what sort of praxis can be made out of this? Even if it is the only practicable method? How could

---

[142] Sigmund Freud, "Negation," *The* Standard Edition of the Complete Psychological Works of Sigmund Freud, Vol. XIX, trans. James Strachey (London: Hogarth Press, 1971)

this kind of listening not fall prey to tendentious pranks of the drives, turning into what Freud characterized as "wild analysis"? Or to something comparably bad, to the master's discourse of standardization, to a doctrine of the primacy of the ego and the disinvestment of desire. Psychoanalysis must answer at every ethical crossroad, or it fails to exist.)

Even a decade later, this effort to take the necessary step to adopt free association was obviously a personal struggle for Freud ("While I was thus at a loss, I clung…"); the interlude of this dark struggle to come to terms with purposeful limits to listening to the patient's associations, is only few pages long, before he seems to swing back into form, confident once again through this remarkable lecture in the results produced by his method.

Why must he allow us to see how he once struggled to fully grasp what he had discovered? He holds, as if it were an article of faith, a prejudice he feels was "useful." But in retrospect, what emerges from the earliest years of psychoanalysis and is carried in full blossom in his metaphysical writings – Freud's bias, which is clearly more of the nature of an axiom – is that the psychical *dispositif* is deterministic. And it cannot be "a little deterministic," as our patients might have it. Nothing happens arbitrarily in the mind. Nothing can be spoken that is unrelated to what precisely cannot (yet) be said. The conscious mind loves to marvel at a flash of insight; yet its most vivid scenes lie within the darkness of unknown contingency.

Would it be erroneous to call determinism, for Freud, a kernel of received truth, and thus an absolute or a reductive generality? Yes, because for Freud this kernel is not "received" but inscribed in the real of the symptom. It is, rather, "registered" with a traumatic mark of particularity, determined by a position in language, and encountered precisely in what has become peculiar to the "sayings" of the subject.

Finally, what could this word, "volition," ever mean for Freud? It must be expressed as what sounds like an oxymoron: it is *unconscious volition*. Psychical reality is for Freud comprised by contending agencies of representation and libido. Volition is a useful notion for the ego, perhaps, and as such perhaps serves the aims of the pleasure principle, but it is not a term Freud seems to have used. His interest in this direction was arrested perhaps by insoluble questions regarding the much simpler concept of "attention."

Freud does, I think, imply in *Totem and Taboo*[143] and other writings that the initiation of both culture and repression by exogamy "lie" in the service of the non-choice of the law, established through transgression, policed through guilt and serving as ritualized destinations for libido – what sort of alternative to a severe and deviously manifest determinism could there possibly be?

Nostalgia, or the past idealized through narcissism, and freedom, what Foucault called "a lifestyle accessory," are devices, surely, of a subject steeped in the non-choices of language. In analysis it can become clear that whatever "outcome" we choose to identify, it is a replacement, a facsimile, a semblant for something else, in a chain of "once-upon-a-time-things," and "once-again-things," linked ultimately to the primal theft, when the object was first born through the (f)act of its disappearance. Eventually, does

---

[143] Sigmund Freud, Totum and Taboo, The Standard Edition of the Complete Psychological
Works of Sigmund Freud, Vol. XIII, trans. James Strachey (London: Hogarth Press, 1971).

this open the door for something that appears in the failure of choice, arriving with the analytic act: the small object *a*?

iii

It seems to come as a hard fiction – a friction – to many, unacceptable, indigestible – even to some analysts – that psychoanalysis finds so little use for the concept of "free will." A question of volition is, of course, central to what I am calling Freud's bias or symptom – his "compromise" to believe without sufficient proof that precisely nothing psychical can be arbitrary. There is no thing that can be predetermined by the ego, nothing decided or conceived in the saying of the patient that is not a matter made contingent by the unconscious – that is not *the matter* in disguise, sexual to the core – displaced in its metonymy, condensed through metaphor, ciphered as determined by the symptomatic structure.

However, for Freud, although determinism in this sense is implicit throughout his thought, this can only remain in the neighborhood of a strong conviction, which in terms of a theoretical science is little more than a hunch. The Freudian approach, which is strongly empirical, uses observations from his clinic that are layered and condensed in experience, then extrapolated into his theories, and which are then explicated into individual case studies. Because the deterministic element in the psychical structure is an effect of language, it wasn't until Lacan reexamined the texts of Freud with the insights of breakthroughs in 20th century linguistic science and sources such as Claude Lévi-Strauss' development of structural anthropology that the deterministic implications of psychoanalysis could be shown. What was a bias for Freud was revealed to be inexorably the case, as demonstrated through a logical analysis of the effects of signifiers.

"Everything emerges from the structure of the signifier," says Lacan near the end of his eleventh seminar, *The Four Fundamental Concepts of Psychoanalysis*[144]. Foremost, this includes the subject himself:

The signifier...makes manifest the subject of its signification. But it functions as a signifier only to reduce the subject in question to being no more than a signifier, to petrify the subject in the same movement in which it calls the subject to function, to speak, as subject.[145]

And, most succinctly:

...a signifier is that which represents a subject *for another signifier.*[146]

How is the existential comforter in the notion of "free will" not the ego's cloaking of its own marionette-strings?

In even his earliest work, Lacan illustrates how the infant is to its essence captured, in a deterministic sense, within the symbolic order.[147][15] This "work" of castration now involves a being who is subjected, from here on out, by a descent, in the sense of an operational legacy. "Chance," as it operates in the world external to the subject, has no further function in the psychical order. What event or trauma can be comparable to the inception of what Lacan calls "unary trait," as the experience of the subject is subsequently circumscribed within its set of linguistic limitations?

---

[144] [12] Jacques Lacan, *The Four Fundamental Concepts of Psychoanalysis*, translated by Alan Sheridan, W.W. Norton 1981, p. 206.

[145] Ibid, p. 207.

[146] Ibid, p. 207.

[147] See, for example, Jacques Lacan, "The Mirror Stage as Formatie of the *I* Function as Revealed in Psychoanalytic Experience," *Ecrits,* translated by Bruce Fink, W.W. Norton, 2006.

And thus, logically speaking, what "choice," in the common sense of a decision made by an ego that discriminates based on "self-interest" – or what sort of "will" that is "free" could operate uncircumscribed by the initial mark left by the imposition of language upon the subject who must speak? To be subjected to speech, as if by choice. To *choose* is to be sundered. And thus to be chosen, or not to be, innumerable times, as the subject of a false choice, this, for Lacan, operates in the order of the *automaton,* "that is, the network of signifiers."[148]

By contrast, chance, as such, can only be attributable to the real. This is the order of what Lacan calls *tuché*.

The function of the *tuché,* of the real as encounter, first presented itself in the history of psycho-analysis in a form of the trauma. Is it not remarkable that, at the origin of the analytic experience, the real should have presented itself in the form of that which is *unassimilable* in it – in the form of the trauma…We are now at the heart of what may enable us to understand the radical character of the conflictual notion introduced by the opposition of the pleasure principle and the reality principle – which is why we cannot conceive the reality principle as having, by virtue of its ascendancy, the last word.[149]

It may be said that, for Freud and Lacan alike, the last word – as is the first – is "spoken" by the drives.[150]

---

[148] Jacques Lacan, *The Four Fundamental Concepts of Psychoanalysis,* translated by Alan Sheridan, W.W. Norton 1981, p. 52

[149] Ibid, p. 55

[150] Or "drive," specifically the death drive, as Lacan speculates for example in Seminar VII, *The Ethics of Psychoanalysis, 1959-60.* Trans. Dennis Porter, W. W. Norton 1992, p. 211-212

Bibliography

Sigmund Freud, "Mourning and Melancholia," *The Standard Edition of the Complete Psychological Works of Sigmund Freud, Vol.* XIV, trans. James Strachey (London: Hogarth Press, 1957)

Sigmund Freud, "On Transience," *The Standard Edition of the Complete Psychological Works of Sigmund Freud, Vol.* XIV, trans. James Strachey (London: Hogarth Press, 1957)

Sigmund Freud, "Thoughts for the Times on War and Death," *The Standard Edition of the Complete Psychological Works of Sigmund Freud, Vol.* XIV, trans. James Strachey (London: Hogarth Press, 1957)

Sigmund Freud, "Papers on Technique," *The Standard Edition of the Complete Psychological Works of Sigmund Freud, Vol.* XII, trans. James Strachey (London: Hogarth Press, 1957)

Colette Solar, *Lacanian Affects,* translated by Bruce Fink, (Routledge, 2016)

Made in the USA
Middletown, DE
29 August 2023

37402965R00071